The Certainty of the SECOND COMING

To order additional copies of
The Certainty of the Second Coming,
by E. Edward Zinke,
call **1-800-765-6955.**

Visit our website at *www.rhpa.org*
for information on other
Review and Herald products.

The Certainty of the SECOND COMING

E. Edward Zinke and
Roland R. Hegstad

REVIEW AND HERALD® PUBLISHING ASSOCIATION
HAGERSTOWN, MD 21740

Copyright © 2000 by
Review and Herald® Publishing Association
International copyright secured

The authors assume full responsibility for the accuracy of all facts and quotations as cited in this book.

Unless otherwise noted, Scripture references are from the New King James Version. Copyright © 1979, 1980, 1982 by Thomas Nelson, Inc. Used by permission. All rights reserved.

Bible texts credited to Phillips are from J. B. Phillips: *The New Testament in Modern English,* Revised Edition. © J. B. Phillips 1958, 1960, 1972. Used by permission of Macmillan Publishing Co.

This book was
Edited by Gerald Wheeler
Copyedited by Jocelyn Fay and James Cavil
Designed by Bill Kirstein
Cover design by PierceCreative/Matthew Pierce
Electronic makeup by Shirley M. Bolivar
Typeset: Bembo 11/12.5

PRINTED IN U.S.A.

04 03 02 01 00   5 4 3 2 1

R&H Cataloging Service
Zinke, Ernest Edward, 1945-
    The certainty of the second coming, by E. Edward Zinke and Roland R. Hegstad.

    1. Second Coming. I. Hegstad, Roland R, joint author. II. Title

ISBN 0-8280-1447-7

Contents

Foreword 7

Introduction 9

Chapter 1 Is Christianity Christian? 13

Chapter 2 The Authority of the Bible and the Certainty of the Second Coming 23

Chapter 3 Creation and the Certainty of the Second Coming 37

Chapter 4 Of Relative Truths and Redemptive Symbols, *by Roland R. Hegstad* 46

Chapter 5 The First Coming Prepares for the Second Coming 58

Chapter 6 Salvation and the Certainty of the Second Coming 69

Chapter 7 The Sanctuary and the Second Coming 79

Chapter 8 Such a Cloud of Witnesses and the Second Coming 90

Chapter 9 The Witness of the Remnant and the Second Coming 101

Chapter 10 Should Our Nineteenth-Century Prophetic Schema Be Revised? *by Roland R. Hegstad* . . 113

Chapter 11 The Certainty of the Second Coming 125

Chapter 12 The Millennium, the Destruction of the Wicked, and the New Earth 133

Chapter 13 God Reveals His Righteousness 146

Foreword

Projects like this do not simply drop out of the sky. I would like to give special thanks to individuals who have navigated with me down the path of life. To my parents, Dr. David and Maxine Zinke, thank you for providing a solid Christian background with an Adventist education and mission field experience. To Jon Dybdahl, a fellow student at Pacific Union College, I deeply appreciate your influence in my decision to prepare for the ministry. To Professors Carl Coffman, Edward Heppenstall, Graham Maxwell, Mervyn Maxwell, Wilbur Alexander, Gerhard Hasel, Raoul Dederen, and my major professor for my Ph.D. program, Dr. William Shea (the same name, but a different teacher from the one who taught at Andrews University and later served in the Biblical Research Institute)—each of you and many others have had an impact on my life. Some inspired me, some provided a spiritual model, some challenged me intellectually, and some provided a strong biblical foundation. I am also indebted to Gordon Hyde, my former boss at the Biblical Research Institute at the General Conference. You gave me the guidance and freedom to utilize and develop my God-given talents. To Roland Hegstad—thank you for your boundless creativity and for helping me meet my deadline by writing two of the chapters. And to the members of my Sabbath school at the Spencerville, Maryland, Seventh-day Adventist Church, thank you for your energetic and enlightening discussions. I have learned much and benefited greatly from each of you.

To Donna Boswell, who deserves major credit for her tireless effort in the preparation of the manuscript. Day after day you responded with a pleasant smile to the columns of work placed on your desk. Kelly Parsley, thank you for keeping the computer viruses at bay, and for destroying them when they did attack. To my sons David and Doug, and their wives, Heidi and Christy, thank you for your support. To Devin, my youngest son, I thank you for checking by my office every evening to see how things were going. And to my wife, Ann—thank you for your endless love and dedication and for sacrificing your organized office so I could have a tidy and efficient place to work (no comments on my office, please).

When all is said and done, if there are any thoughts worthwhile, the praise and honor go to our Lord and Saviour. May this book provide a stepping-stone to a closer walk with Him.

Introduction

You have just received an official-looking envelope from the United Nations. With anticipation you tear it open. Excitement runs through your veins as you read the invitation to join the first international space team to land on the planet Mars. It will be a select, highly trained group of five individuals. Immediately calling your closest friends and relatives to inform them of the honor, you can hardly stop talking about it. Nothing so exciting has ever happened to you before.

Liftoff will take place in six months. The preparation will be intense. Briefings will take place on everything from the scientific experiments the crew will conduct to the physical and mental preparation necessary to survive the trip. Trainers will teach you to handle weightlessness, how to eat with a space suit on, how to sleep, and how to be productive in the environment expected on Mars. Quickly you realize that the upcoming event will dominate every minute of your life. Getting the proper food, rest, exercise, and training will all center on the moment of takeoff. The voyage will affect the way you use your time, the things that you think about, and even how you relate to other people. Being among the first to step foot on Mars will largely define who you are as a person.

Each of us has received a similar invitation, not from the United Nations, but from the King of the universe. And it involves not a short-term event, but eternity! Can anything be more exciting than our invitation from the Creator to explore with Him the vastness and the intricacies of the universe that He has made and to live throughout eternity in His fellowship and that of our loved ones?

Would we find an offer from the United Nations more captivating than one from the Lord of the universe? Would the opportunity to be among the first humans to reach Mars be of greater significance than our invitation to the marriage supper of the Lamb? Would preparation for a Mars landing be of more importance in defining who we are than the hope of the Second Coming? If so, has the Second Coming lost something of its certainty, its urgency, its reality, and therefore its ability to shape our lives?

This book seeks to reinvigorate your appreciation of the greatest space event of all time. The invitation has been delivered with special care through prophets, apostles, and God's own Son, Jesus Christ. It did not come in an envelope delivered by an impersonal postal carrier, but rather from the outstretched arms of God Himself, who longs to welcome you home.

God's invitation to come home is not simply an event to add to the 29 other items already on your calendar! It is the event of the ages—the culmination of all that God has done to reconcile us to Himself. When you accept God's invitation, its magnitude will take center stage in your life. It will dominate your thinking, the use of your time, and your personal relationships, and it will cement your relationship with God for eternity.

As we study together the certainty of the Second Coming, we will attempt to explore its relationship to all aspects of our lives. We will examine the three angels' messages to find out how God's entire biblical message relates to the Second Coming. As we do so we will discover that the doctrine of the Second Coming intertwines with many other doctrines, and that if we begin to question any fundamental Bible doctrine, we will also raise questions about all others.

Since we will be examining Bible doctrine from the perspective of the Second Coming, we will also step back for a moment to explore the meaning of doctrine itself. Doctrine is not an end within itself, but an essential element in establishing our relationship with God. What is central to Christianity is the message that we can be reconciled to God through Jesus Christ. The culmination of our reconciliation takes place at the Second Coming.

Doctrine is meaningful when it plays its role in our restoration to God. Some might argue that the biblical emphasis that Christianity is a relationship with God negates the importance of doctrinal and lifestyle issues. However, we will see that our relationship with God does not do away with law and doctrine—rather, as Paul says, it establishes them (Rom. 3:31). May this book be a guide to prepare us to participate in the greatest event of all time! By God's grace, let us all be members of the same exploratory team so that we may set foot on Planet Heaven together.

Chapter 1

Is Christianity Christian?

SIMEON STYLITES was a very dedicated Christian who lived in the fifth century A.D. Upon his conversion from paganism, he desired to make a total commitment to the Christian faith. He wanted to understand its essence, its meaning, so that he could devote his life to it. Immediately selling his large inherited estate, he set aside enough to sustain his sister and donated the remainder to the church. Then he committed his life to monasticism.

Withdrawing in seclusion to a cave near his native village, he devoted himself to meditation. Soon disciples gathered around him and nearby villagers crowded in to be close to the pious monk. In order to escape the world, he moved farther into the wilderness and built a tower upon which to live. When his disciples erected towers around him so that they could share his piety, he constructed even higher towers in order to achieve his goal of piety. According to tradition, he finally lived out his life on a tower 60 feet high—sufficient to separate himself from the world and allow uninterrupted meditation in freedom from the distraction of the crowds below.

Did Simeon find the true substance of Christianity? What lies at the core of Christianity?

What Is Christianity?

People understand Christianity in many different ways. For some, it is a legal religion. Obey its laws, and you are a Christian. Keep the commandments, pay tithe (add a few extra cents for safety's sake), attend church, eat right—that's what makes Christianity Christian. For others, Christianity is a knowledge religion. If you know that the seventh day is the Sabbath to observe from sundown to sundown, that the dead are not conscious, that the investigative judgment started in heaven in 1844, and that Christ will return soon in a literal, visible manner, then you have achieved Christianity.

Others would see the essence of Christianity in socially correct living—giving to the poor, establishing schools, caring for the homeless, and healing the sick. And some would agree with Simeon that meditation best sums up Christianity.

Each approach demonstrates how far humanity will go in its attempt to find Christianity. It illustrates how hard we will work, think, give, or meditate to achieve our own salvation, to make ourselves presentable to God. If we can only find the right thing to do, then we can be saved and will be ready for the Second Coming.

Paul expresses concern about religion based upon human effort. In Romans 1 he reviews the status of the Gentiles. They have established their religion on human activity. The final result of their human endeavor was the worship of the creature instead of the Creator. Next, in Romans 2, Paul discusses the Jews. Despite the fact that they possessed special revelation from God, they also have sought salvation by works. Finally, in chapter 3, Paul concludes that all have sinned (both Gentile and Jew) and come short of God's glory (Rom. 3:8-18, 23). Therefore, the deeds of the law will justify no one (Rom. 3:20; Gal. 2:16).

Paul has similar concerns for religions based upon wisdom and knowledge. God will destroy the wisdom of even the wisest, for we cannot come to know God through human wisdom (1 Cor. 1:19-25). Instead of affirming a knowledge-based approach to religion, Paul prays that we will instead experience the love of God that surpasses all other knowledge (Eph. 3:19).

Christianity is not a ladder that we use to climb to God or a checklist of do's and don'ts on how to live. Neither can we reduce it to meditation or a list of doctrines. It is not a human philosophy.

The Essence of Christianity

Christ Himself summarized for us the essence of Christianity: "And this is eternal life, that they may know You, the only true

God, and Jesus Christ whom You have sent" (John 17:3). The sum and substance of Christianity is to come to a knowledge of God and Jesus Christ. The word *knowledge* here does not refer to facts and figures, such as the distance between two cities or the substances required to produce soap or the specific parts needed to fix a car. Rather, it involves the kind of knowledge that leads to a personal relationship. The goal of salvation is to enter a full, rewarding, and mature fellowship with God and Jesus Christ.

God created us for communion with Himself. The very first evening of human creation God spent in the garden fellowshipping with Adam and Eve. He made us in His own image, because only thus can we have fellowship with Him. When our character is in harmony with that of God, we can relate to Him with no barrier in between. The Lord desires such close fellowship with us that the Bible often uses the imagery of marriage to describe it. "I am married to you," God declares (Jer. 3:14).

When we are married to the Lord, we "shall know the Lord" (Hosea 2:20). We will enter a personal relationship with Him, the real substance of Christianity. As Christ said, to *know* God is life eternal (John 17:3).

Unfortunately, sin shattered the beautiful picture of life in harmony with God, rupturing face-to-face communion with Him. All have sinned and come short of the glory of God (Rom. 3:23) and we have become "an unclean thing" (Isa. 64:6). Our condition in sin cuts us off from fellowship with the Life-giver. We are like a branch sawed off from the tree, a lightbulb unscrewed from its socket, or a water faucet disconnected from the rest of the plumbing.

Why does sin sever us from God? Because sin is the transgression of the law (1 John 3:4). And why is transgressing the law so dreadful? Because the law is a description of the character of God. It is what God is in His very nature. When we break His law, we are going against His character, and to violate the character of an individual is to distort or break one's relationship with that person. We are not at peace with God, because our characters are out of harmony with His. Furthermore, by going our own way, we have chosen to live *independently* of God (Isa. 53:6). Lost in sin, "we can do nothing, absolutely nothing, to commend ourselves to divine favor. We must not trust at all to ourselves nor to our good works" (*Selected Messages,* book 1, pp. 353, 354). As a result, we cannot rectify our situation with God by our works, knowledge, meditation, or any other human effort.

By ourselves, we are helpless and hopeless. We cannot come to God and say, "Let's be friends and forget the past. Let's build upon our mutual strengths and enjoy each other's fellowship." Nothing within ourselves can commend us to God.

The grace of God is that even while we were sinners—in fact, His enemies—He Himself reached down to us through His own Son, Jesus Christ, in order to reconcile us to Himself. God gave Himself to us in Jesus Christ in order that we may fellowship with Him (Rom. 5:8-11; 1 Cor.1:9). Because of Him we can be grafted back into the Vine, can be adopted into God's family.

The Role of Doctrine and Lifestyle

If the basis of Christianity is entrance into a relationship with God, then what role, if any, do doctrine, the law, meditation, and lifestyle play? Instead of bothering with doctrine, why not simply concentrate on our relationship with God?

Consider some of the elements of a healthy relationship. If I wanted to enter a relationship with you, it would be necessary first of all for me to know something about you as a person. Without such knowledge our relationship would be meaningless. We could sit and stare at each other all day long, but there would be no substance to the relationship. Second, it would be necessary for me to know something about myself. A lack of self-understanding can easily lead to misunderstandings, causing relationships to flounder. Third, we would need to understand the kind of relationship that can appropriately take place between us. The first two points seem obvious enough. Let us illustrate the third. Relationships vary depending upon whether one is relating to a spouse, a son, a daughter, a boss, or a secretary. Each of these relationships is unique, and therefore operates by a different set of guidelines.

Doctrines are essential to our relationship with God, for they provide the information we need to enter into deeper communion with Him. They tell us about God, about ourselves, and how we may appropriately relate to Him. Just as there are various types of unique relationships in the human sphere, so also there is a unique relationship appropriate with God.

What role do law and Christian lifestyle play in our relationship with God? Why not simply focus on the relationship and skip the standards of the Christian church? Because all healthy relationships are based upon clear guidelines. The Bible provides the criteria for living in a loving relationship with God and fellow human beings. Furthermore, since the law describes God's character, abiding by its precepts means that we are living in harmony with the divine character. When our lives harmonize with that of God, then true fellowship is possible with Him.

Paul emphasized that Christ gave Himself for us in order that He might cleanse us and present us to Himself a "glorious church, not having spot or wrinkle . . . that she should be holy and without blemish" (Eph. 5:26, 27). Only then can we truly enter a full relationship with God.

John discusses the role of the law in our relationship with God. He tells us that Christ came into the world to reveal the Father (John 1:18). This eternal life (Christ) was with the Father, and was manifest to us in order that we might have fellowship with both the Father and with His Son Jesus Christ (1 John 1:1-4). "God is light and in Him is no darkness at all. If we say that we have fellowship with Him, and walk in darkness, we lie and do not practice the truth. But as we walk in the light as He is in the light, we have fellowship with one another, and the blood of Jesus Christ His Son cleanses us from all sin" (verses 5-7).

The law is not a burdensome checklist we must follow to obtain salvation. It is a guide to relationship with God. No wonder David declared that his delight was in the law (Ps. 1:2; 119:47, 70, 77, 174).

In summary, Christianity is not Christian if it attempts to find its basis in knowledge of doctrine, works, meditation, or any other human effort. Neither the law nor doctrine is the goal of Christianity. However, they do provide the guidelines and the context within which our relationship with God can flourish.

Christianity is fulfilled when we are restored to a right relationship with God through Christ. It means that Christ is the center of doctrine, not simply because the study of the doctrine refers to His name, nor because His words are quoted when teaching doctrine, but because doctrine leads to knowledge of Him so that we might fellowship with Him.

Throughout this book it will be one of our goals to understand how particular doctrines enable a fuller understanding of and relationship with God. Let us illustrate this briefly with the doctrine of the Second Coming.

Communion With Jesus and the Second Coming

Someone once asked a number of individuals in a Sabbath school class what they thought of when they contemplated the Second Coming and heaven. A number of things immediately came to mind: its glory, the fact that it would be visible worldwide, and that God would resurrect the righteous dead and they would join the righteous living on a journey to heaven. Heaven engendered visions of mansions, streets of gold, unbelievably beautiful gardens, and pet lions. Momentary silence followed, then someone spoke up. "You know what I long for most when I think of the Second Coming—communion with Jesus, my Saviour!"

The goal of Christianity is to be restored to a right relationship with God. Its culmination will take place at the Second Coming when we will have face-to-face communion with God. We have seen that Scripture often compares the Christian life with marriage to God. Since the Second Coming is the climax of our relationship with God, it is only natural that the Bible should also describe it as a marriage. Christ used the parables of the wedding banquet (Matt. 22:1-14; Luke 14:15-24) and the 10 bridesmaids (Matt. 25:1-13) and the analogy of the groomsman (Mark 2:18-20; Matt. 9:14, 15; Luke 5:33-35) to depict various aspects of the Second Coming. John the revelator employed the same imagery: "'Let us be glad and rejoice and give him glory, for the marriage of the Lamb has come, and his wife has made herself ready.' And to her it was granted to be arrayed in fine linen, clean and bright, for the fine linen is the righteous acts of the saints. Then he said to me, 'Write: "Blessed are those who are called to the marriage supper of the Lamb!"'" (Rev. 19:7-9).

The Second Coming is a time of rejoicing, not only for the saints, but also for God! "As the bridegroom rejoices over the bride, so shall your God rejoice over you" (Isa. 62:5). One of the greatest sorrows in any relationship is the pain of separation—the end of a family visit, the death of a loved one, or divorce. One of the joys of salvation is that the Second Coming marks the beginning of an eternal relationship with God in which we will never feel the pain of separation again.

We may delineate the events just before and after the Second Coming and describe its exact manner. All these biblical teachings are essential. But if we forget the central fact that it is Jesus who is returning, we have missed the whole point.

The doctrine of the Second Coming tells us that Christ is Lord and King, our Saviour and our Judge. It reminds us that we are His subjects, and that were it not for His salvation, we would stand under His condemnation. God is not only the almighty, all-knowing, everywhere-present ruler of the universe, but He is a personal God who is coming to completely restore us to Himself so that He might take us home to live with Him throughout eternity. The promise of His soon return fills us with hope in the present and dominates our lives as we look forward to His coming. If we emphasize only the details of the Second Coming, as important as they are, and miss the God revealed to us in the doctrine, we are majoring in minors. We are making the detail of doctrine and the letter of the law the center of our life rather than Jesus Christ.

A Systematic Whole

Just as there is a vital connection between the doctrines and fellowship with God, so also an interrelationship exists between the doctrines themselves. They are a systematic whole. Sometimes we succumb to the temptation to look at doctrine in isolation from other aspects of Christianity. Often we separate the doctrines from each other. We may attempt to pick and choose among the doctrines. For example, some say that we can accept the Sabbath and the Second Coming doctrines, but we do not need to hold to a literal 24-hour consecutive six-day Creation week.

"The precious, golden links of truth are not separate, detached, disconnected doctrines; but link after link form one string of golden truth, and constitute a complete whole, with Christ as its living center" (*Appeal and Suggestions to Conference Officers*, p. 26).

Come with me to a beautiful white sandy beach. Majestic rocky cliffs tower on each side of us. The waves roll onto the beach in front of us while they crash against the rocks along the cliffs. Clouds painted red and orange by the setting sun fleece the sky. The rays of the sun glisten in the wet sand and sparkle in the splashing waves. Lean back on the beach and enjoy the sight.

Now watch as the scene changes. You are sitting in the same place, looking at the same beach and rocks and waves, but the sun has vanished. The sky is dark and gray. The sand does not glisten; no pink tints the sky. Although you have not moved, are you looking at the same picture?

Biblical doctrine must be viewed as a whole. When we remove from it even one of the basic fundamental doctrines, it is as if we have erased the sun from the picture. We might be sitting in the same place, but the picture is not the same. All biblical doctrines comprise a beautiful mosaic. To extract even one piece of the picture spoils the whole.

Doctrine and Relation to God

Doctrine also plays an important part in the Christian life, because it has a direct impact on character. It is a law of the mind and character that they form according to the thing or person that we respect most in life. If we admire God supremely, and if our conception of God is one true to His character, it will transform our lives in harmony with His. This in turn will allow a closer walk with Him. But if our conception of God is false, and we admire that false image so that it dominates our lives, our character will then begin to reflect our false view of God. This will result in distortion if not destruction of our relationship with God, for our character will not harmonize with His. Furthermore, just as misunderstanding the character of another person leads to a misconception of that individual, so also a misunderstanding of the nature of God leads to a confused relationship with Him. Thus biblical doctrine plays a key role in our relationship with God, for it brings us His revelation of Himself.

John says that eternal life comes from knowing the only "true" God. Not just any god, not a deity created from our own imagination—a "designer God"—but God as He has revealed Himself to us in the living Word, Jesus Christ (John 1:18), and in His written Word, the Bible. Ellen White also makes this point, "Wonderful, wonderful words, almost beyond comprehension! Will the teachers in our schools understand this? Will they take the word of God as the lesson book able to make them wise unto salvation? This book is the voice of God speaking to us. The Bible opens to us the words of life; for it makes us acquainted with Christ who is our life. In order to have true, abiding faith in Christ, we must know Him as He is *represented* in the word" (*Fundamentals of Christian Education,* p. 433; italics supplied).

Through the Word of God we may begin fellowship with God now. "As he [the Christian] studies and meditates upon the themes into which 'the angels desire to look,' he may have their companionship. . . . He may dwell in this world in the atmosphere of heaven, imparting to earth's sorrowing and tempted ones thoughts of hope and longings for holiness; himself coming closer and still closer into fellowship with the Unseen; like him of old who walked with God, drawing nearer and nearer the threshold of the eternal world, until the portals shall open, and he shall enter there. He will find himself no stranger. The voices that will greet him are the voices of the holy ones, who, unseen, were on earth his companions—voices that here he learned to distinguish and to love. He who through the word of God has lived in fellowship with Heaven will himself be at home in heaven's companionship" (*My Life Today,* p. 264).

John did not say that we should know God by whatever we think He is! Nor did he suggest that we should get to know some designer god. He emphasized that we should know the only "true" God! Preparing for the Second Coming is not like getting ready for a blind date. Nor is it like marriage on the Internet. It is preparation for marriage with someone we already know because we have met Him in the doctrines revealed in His Word, someone with whom we desire to spend eternity because of what we already know about Him.

Biblical doctrine is important, for it leads us to a knowledge of God, who is coming to take us home with Himself. However, we must be cautious not to make doctrine an end in itself. Knowledge of doctrine is not the goal of Christianity, but a means to an end—to a full, meaningful, joyful relationship with God and Jesus Christ.

Suppose that someone had told me about my wife-to-be, Ann, before I became personally acquainted with her. They could have extolled her beauty, housekeeping ability, cooking skills, and lovely personality. Or they might have emphasized what a good mother she would make. But however helpful their most detailed description of her might have been, it would never have substituted for getting acquainted with Ann herself.

Throughout the Bible God has revealed Himself to us in teachings we call doctrine. They tell us about the only true God in detail. Yet, however important they are to our knowledge of God, we must never make them an end within themselves. We must open our lives to their teachings, in order that we might come to know God and Jesus Christ in person Themselves, whom to know is life eternal!

Chapter 2

The Authority of the Bible and the Certainty of the Second Coming

I WAS STANDING in front of a large commemorative boulder situated at the center of a quiet intersection in the city of Constance, Germany. The cobblestone roundabout gave way to landscaping that accentuated the large stone boulder. On one side of the boulder was engraved the name John Huss. The other side bore the name Jerome.

Huss and Jerome had been professors at the university of Prague in Bohemia. Their participation in the Protestant Reformation brought their teaching and preaching into question by the church at Rome. The authorities therefore summoned them to appear before the Council of Constance.

Just prior to my visit to the commemorative boulder, I had toured the site of their house arrest and had driven by the council chamber where the authorities had tried and convicted them as criminals for their allegiance to the Bible as the Word of God. I then visited a tower protruding out of Lake Constance where they might have been imprisoned in the basement the night before their execution. If so, they would have been standing waist deep in the glacial waters of the lake.

I was now deep in contemplation as I stood by the memorial boulder, the place of their execution. The words of Ellen White rang in my mind: "God will have a people upon the earth to maintain the Bible, and the Bible only, as the standard of all doctrines and the basis of all reforms" (*The Great Controversy,* p. 595). What would it be like to give up one's life rather than to compromise the authority of the Bible?

After several minutes of meditation, as a good tourist, I pulled out my camera to record the event. I had been so deep in meditation that I did not notice until that moment that an elderly woman sat on a park bench at the base of the boulder. The camera startled her. She stood up, circled the rock two or three times while nervously looking back and forth between the camera and the boulder, and finally, shaking her head, took off down the street at what seemed like her top speed.

I pictured her as a young girl growing up in that city, possibly living just several doors down from the monument. Perhaps she played hide-and-seek around the boulder, tossed a ball back and forth with the boys on one of the quiet side streets adjoining it, or sat on the park bench next to it while resting in its shade. And yet she had somehow never understood its significance—a commemoration of two lives snuffed out as they burned at the stake for their allegiance to the Word of God.

Sola Scriptura

My thoughts then shifted to our church. We inherited the emphasis of the Reformation—*sola scriptura*. The Bible alone was our creed. This solid rock was in our own backyard. We grew up with it, played around it, stood upon it, sat on the bench beside it, and rested in its shade—and yet, with all of this familiarity, did we truly understand its significance?

As Seventh-day Adventists we were the people of the Book. We built upon it and relied on it completely, for we were hammering out the doctrines of the Sabbath, the state of the dead, and the judgment—all biblical doctrines based upon the authority of the Bible. But we simply assumed its authority, since the issue was not in question. Our concern was to emphasize the biblical doctrines that had been lost to the Christian church.

The Authority of the Bible

Adventists came out of churches that had already accepted the authority of the Bible and the Reformation call to *sola scriptura* (the Bible alone) as well as *sola fide* (by faith alone). We simply assumed that the Bible was the sole foundational authority and that salvation was by faith alone. Having assumed these foundational doctrines, we moved on to the task of restoring the rest of biblical teaching. As a result, we did not come to terms with the issues involved in either doctrine. Therefore, we were vulnerable to salvation by works and to human reason as the foundation of theology.

Our first crisis came with the doctrine of righteousness by faith. As we all know, in 1888 we confronted it head-on. What had been assumed now had to be spelled out clearly. The doctrine has been renewed from time to time within the church and has been a blessing both to the church as a whole and to each of us individually. We can be grateful for the many voices that have joined in the proclamation of salvation by grace through faith.

Just as we faced a crisis in the doctrine of righteousness by faith, so we also encounter a similar crisis on the authority of the Bible. And just as we became aware of the issues and principles involved in *sola fide,* so we must also grasp those involved in the doctrine of *sola scriptura.* We can be grateful for the many voices in our church that are beginning to understand and proclaim the message that the Bible is the sole foundation of our faith.

Many similarities exist between the doctrines of *sola fide* and *sola scriptura.* Just as salvation is a gift, so too the Bible as God's self-revelation is also a gift. And as we must not manipulate salvation through human effort, so we must not control the Bible by human reason. We must receive both salvation and the Bible by faith alone.

The history of theology reminds us that when one principle is lost, the other eventually disappears also. The "giveness" of salvation depends upon the "giveness" of Scripture, for if the authority of Scripture rests upon human works of reason, then the salvation of which the Bible speaks also arises from those same human works.

Misunderstanding Biblical Authority

As I have thought back on that moment of meditation by the Huss and Jerome memorial, I have realized that just as the elderly woman sitting on the park bench by the boulder missed the significance of the memorial stone, so in many ways I too have failed to grasp the meaning of the authority of the Bible.

For example, at times I have sought an absolute rock-solid foundation to put under the Bible so that I could accept it as the Word of God and therefore the only authority. I wanted to use the power of science, archaeology, history, and philosophy to build that foundation. I thought that such approaches would confirm that the Bible is the absolute authority. But I did not realize that I had just made myself the absolute authority. I rested my case on the excellency of reason rather than on the power of the Word of God.

Also I have misunderstood the authority of the Bible by seeking a "balanced" theology. I attempted to balance law and grace, faith and reason, and natural revelation with special revelation. Somehow I overlooked the fact that what might appear balanced to me might be altogether unbalanced from God's standpoint, and that it was the biblical message that was important rather than what seemed appropriate from my human perspective. Furthermore, some truths are not a question of balance, but a question of relationship. It is foolish for the housewife to argue with the architect of her new home over the balance between the kitchen and the foundation. That is a question of relationship. The kitchen must rest upon the foundation. So the keeping of the law follows salvation by grace, reason rests upon faith, and natural revelation is understood within the context of special revelation.

I misunderstood the authority of the Bible when I wanted to find the "truth," wherever it may be found, whether it be in nature, reason, science, philosophy, history, or elsewhere. I sought to find the truth so that I could find my own way to God. I was acting as if "truth" somehow had an existence independent of God and His Word. Like Pilate, I was asking, "What is truth?" (John 18:38) when the "way, the truth and the life" (John 14:6) was standing directly before me! For me, truth was a thing, or a concept, by which I would measure everything, including God and His Word.

Also I failed to grasp the authority of the Bible when I wanted to take the "truths" discovered in the natural world and synthesize them with the truths from Scripture. Without realizing it, I was using a method that came from the major theologian of the Middle Ages, Thomas Aquinas. For him, theology rested upon the Bible *and* nature, the Bible *and* reason, and the Bible *and* church tradition. In a sense, I was saying, it is wiser to build the house upon the rock *and* the sand.

Thus I misunderstood the authority of the Bible when I saw it as just one among many others. I thought in terms of the *primacy*, or the *supremacy,* of the Bible rather than in terms of its sole foundational authority. It shocked me when I discovered my position on the *primacy* of Scripture to be the pre-Reformation view that the Reformation answered with the principle of *sola scriptura*.

As a result I compromised the authority of the Bible by assuming the contemporary humanistic concept of freedom—that we are absolutely free in the universe to make our decision either for or against Christ from a neutral starting point. The biblical teaching is that we are either slaves of Christ or slaves of Satan, and that we are set free only when we come to Christ.

Finally, I ignored the authority of the Bible when I wanted to meet people where they are in order to bring them to Christ. I sought to start with their worldview, with their philosophical framework, in order to convince them of the truth of Scripture. In so doing, I was setting their culture up as the final authority. While it is true that we must meet people in such a way that they can understand the message of the gospel, the conviction must come from the Holy Spirit, not from the dictates of their own culture. Our task is to confront their culture with God's Word, rather than to base their acceptance of God's Word upon their particular culture.

Without verbalizing it, I was trying to tell Him where He fits into the organization of knowledge. I was attempting to bring Him into the canon of truth. How lucky God was that I was on the scene to pull together the best arguments to prove His existence and defend the Bible as His Word. I wanted a designer god who fit my culture and rationality.

In many ways I was like doctors who lay their patients out on the operating table, examine them, anesthetize them so that they can control them, breathe life into their bodies, massage their heart, map their brain waves, excise a portion of their organs for further examination, diagnose them, fix their problems if possible, and finally piece their bodies back together as best they can. I failed to recognize that the process is just the opposite—that I must be the one placed upon the table. I must submit to the control of the Word of God, be dissected by it, allow its power under the Holy Spirit to be breathed into me, and thus be healed by it.

The Bible and Other Authorities

A major theme runs throughout *The Great Controversy:* That God has had His people throughout the ages who have upheld the twin truths of *sola fide* (salvation by faith alone), and *sola scriptura* (by the Bible alone), and God will have a people on earth at the end of time who will proclaim the same truths against all other authorities, whether they be ecclesiastical, political, existential, or rational.

During the Middle Ages, just as church teachers conceived of salvation as based upon faith *and* works, so the formula for theology was the Bible *and* church tradition, the Bible *and* nature, the Bible *and* reason, and the Bible *and* philosophy. While they upheld the *supremacy* or *primacy* of Scripture, they placed it alongside other "lesser" authorities. The net result was that they actually compromised the Bible's authority.

The Reformation responded to the notion that the Bible was to be placed alongside something else with the principle of *sola scriptura*. The Bible alone was the basis not only of theology, but also for every other aspect of our lives, including the foundation of our intellect and knowledge.

Science has had a profound impact upon modern culture. Its successes have, at least until recently, made it the foundation for all intellectual activity, including religion. Thus it might be tempting to say that if reason is not the foundation, then it has no role at all. While the Reformation made the Bible rather than reason the foundation of thought, it did not deny that God spoke through other channels, such as the church or nature. The Bible, however, was the authority to determine when and where God had spoken elsewhere. Neither did the Reformation deny that human reason had a significant role to play. *Reason was a legitimate tool for understanding when it operated from the foundation of the Bible.*

We might illustrate the relationship between reason and the Bible by considering the various aspects of my house. A set of plans guided its construction, and the entire structure rests upon a foundation. My house also has a living room, kitchen, bedrooms, doors, and windows. It would not be a house if it did not have these elements. But my house would collapse if I turned it upside down in attempt to place it on the roof instead of on the foundation! So our lives consist of many elements: reason, the five senses, emotions, social relations, spirituality, and so on. All of them are essential to living a full life. However, if we make one of the other elements the guide or foundation in place of the Bible, our lives will collapse. We will bow down before a designer god of our own making instead of to the God who has revealed Himself.

Bible as the Word of God

The Reformation's return to the authority of Scripture did not arise out of philosophical considerations. It came out of a recognition of the biblical claim to be the Word of God and of a desire to submit to that Word. A constant theme throughout the Bible is that its message is the Word of God brought to us by prophets and apostles. "For prophecy never came by the will of man, but holy men of God spoke as they were moved by the Holy Spirit" (2 Peter 1:21). "All Scripture is given by inspiration of God" (2 Tim. 3:16). Moses brought "all these words which the Lord commanded him" (Ex. 19:7). "And God spoke all these words, saying:" (Ex. 20:1). "Moses wrote all the words of the Lord" (Ex. 24:4; cf. 25:21; 34:27; Lev. 26:46; Deut. 4:5, 14); "Thus says the Holy One of Israel" (Isa. 30:12; cf. 1:1, 2; Jer. 30:2; 36:1, 2, 27, 28; Eze. 11:25; Zech. 4:8). "When you received the word of God which you heard from us, you welcomed it not as the word of men, but as it is in truth, the word of God" (1 Thess. 2:13). "The Revelation of Jesus Christ, which God gave Him to show His servants—things which must shortly take place. And He sent and signified it by His angel to His servant John, who bore witness to the word of God, and to the testimony of Jesus Christ, to all things that he saw" (Rev. 1:1, 2; cf. verses 11, 17-19; 2:7). Such passages offer just a sampling of the many times that the Bible writers declared their message to be the word of the Lord.

In a number of places both Bible writers and Christ Himself referred to other portions of the Bible as the Word of God. "The Lord testified against Israel and against Judah, by all of His prophets" (2 Kings 17:13). "They made their hearts like flint, refusing to hear the law and the words which the Lord of hosts had sent by His Spirit through the former prophets" (Zech. 7:12). While quoting from the book of Exodus, Christ said, "Have you not read what was spoken to you by God" (Matt. 22:31, 32). Zacharias referred to the promises of God that "He [God] spoke by the mouth of His holy prophets, who have been since the world began" (Luke 1:70). In his sermon on the day of Pentecost, Peter said, "This Scripture had to be fulfilled, which the Holy Spirit spoke before by the mouth of David" (Acts 1:16; cf. 28:25; Heb. 3:7).

Peter also declared that God revealed His message of salvation through prophets even though they may not have understood the message themselves. "Of this salvation the prophets have inquired and searched carefully, who prophesied of the grace *that would come* to you, searching what, or what manner of time, the Spirit of Christ who was in them was indicating when He testified beforehand the sufferings of Christ and the glories that would follow. To them it was revealed that, not to themselves, but to us they were ministering the things which now have been reported to you through those who have preached the gospel to you by the Holy Spirit sent from heaven—things which angels desire to look into" (1 Peter 1:10-12). The book of Hebrews affirms that God conveyed His message through the prophets and His Son (Jesus Christ) (Heb. 1:1, 2). Paul refers to the Scriptures as the "Oracles of God" (Rom. 3:2; Heb. 5:12).

Christ Himself verified His own mission by Scripture. "For if you believed Moses, you would believe Me; for he wrote about Me. But if you do not believe his writings, how will you believe My words?" (John 5:46, 47; cf. 5:39, 40). On the road to Emmaus Jesus used the Scriptures to clarify the significance of His ministry. "And beginning at Moses and all the Prophets, He expounded to them in all the Scriptures the things concerning Himself" (Luke 24:27; cf. 24:44-47).

The Bible is the Word of God given by the will of God through prophets and apostles. It is therefore the authority for our understanding of God and our lives. Christ said, "Scripture cannot be broken" (John 10:35). Isaiah admonished: "To the law and to the testimony! If they do not speak according to this word, it is because there is no light in them" (Isa. 8:20). Paul clearly spelled out the authority of his message: "But even if we, or an angel from heaven, preach any other gospel to you than what we have preached to you, let him be accursed. As we have said before, so now I say again, if anyone preaches any other gospel to you than what you have received, let him be accursed. . . . But I make known to you, brethren, that the gospel which was preached by me is not according to man. For I neither received it from man, nor was I taught it, but it came through the revelation of Jesus Christ" (Gal. 1:8-12). "It is written" was the foundation of the answers that Christ gave to Satan in the wilderness (Matt. 4:4, 7, 10).

Many people view the Bible as they would any other ancient national literature. It is for them a collection of bits and pieces of folk tradition gathered over many generations from various merging cultures. While the Bible might have value as a reflection of the highest example of human spiritual insight, it is not itself the Word of God. Thus, for example, biblical predictions about the Second Coming are little more than the collective dream of past generations.

As we have seen, the Bible does not understand itself as the manifestation of human spiritual genius. Though conveyed through apostles and prophets who themselves used their own language, the Holy Spirit superintended and safeguarded the process in such a way that God conveyed His message to His people. The Bible did not come by human will, but by the will of God. It is a unique piece of literature, for it is the Word of God.

Trying to Find God

Non-Christian religions seek to obtain knowledge of God by

observing the world around them. After considering what they have seen in nature, history, interpersonal relationships, and their own understanding of themselves, they then attempt to deduce a "god" who fits with their understanding of the natural world. If they see the world as harsh, then they regard God as harsh. Should the world seem mysterious, then God is mysterious. And if the world is capricious, then God must be capricious. Sometimes their religion is simple, and they carve an image out of wood to represent their God. Other times their religion is sophisticated, and they build their god out of the philosophy of their age. In either case, their "god" is a deity who fits their observations and beliefs about the nature of the world they see around them. He is a "designer god" that matches their generation. Such representations of God, whether simple or sophisticated, constitute idolatry.

All such approaches leave humanity without a true knowledge of God. "The world through wisdom did not know God" (1 Cor. 1:21). The natural world can reveal His eternal power and Godhead. However, when we attempt to worship God based upon a human interpretation of the natural world, we distort His reality. Turning creation upside down, we worship the creature instead of the Creator. The result is the revelation of the wrath of God (Rom. 1:18-32). By contrast, the gospel reveals the righteousness of God (verses 16, 17)! "Searching the Scriptures alone will bring the knowledge of the true God and Jesus Christ whom He hath sent" (*Fundamentals of Christian Education,* p. 415).

"Human talent and human conjecture have tried by searching to find out God. But guesswork has proved itself to be guesswork. Man cannot by searching find out God. This problem has not been given to human beings. All that man needs to know and can know of God has been revealed in His Word and in the life of His Son, the great Teacher. . . .

"God cannot be understood by men. His ways and works are past finding out. In regard to the revelations that He has made of Himself in His Word, we may talk, but other than this, let us say of Him, Thou art God, and Thy ways are past finding out" (*The Seventh-day Adventist Bible Commentary,* Ellen G. White Comments, vol. 6, p. 1079).

The Bible and Education

Our era has become enamored with science. The scientific method has almost become the god of our age and the foundation of all knowledge. But this humanistic concept of knowledge conflicts with the biblical teaching on the authority of the Bible and its foundational role in our lives—not only spiritually, but also intellectually.

The God who created the universe has given us in the Bible a foundation and guide to understanding that world. "Since God is the source of all true knowledge, it is, as we have seen, the first object of education to direct our minds to His own revelation of Himself. Adam and Eve received knowledge through direct communion with God; and they learned of Him through His works. All created things, in their original perfection, were an expression of the thought of God. To Adam and Eve nature was teeming with divine wisdom. But by transgression man was cut off from learning of God through direct communion and, to a great degree, through His works. The earth, marred and defiled by sin, reflects but dimly the Creator's glory. It is true that His object lessons are not obliterated. Upon every page of the great volume of His created works may still be traced His handwriting. Nature still speaks of her Creator. Yet these revelations are partial and imperfect. And in our fallen state, with weakened powers and restricted vision, we are incapable of interpreting aright. We need the fuller revelation of Himself that God has given in His written Word.

"The Holy Scriptures are the perfect standard of truth, and as such should be given the highest place in education" (*Education*, pp. 16, 17).

The Bible Its Own Interpreter

Although many different individuals participated in bringing the Bible to us, it has only one author, the Holy Spirit. Since it comes from the one author, its message is a unity. Therefore, the Bible must be its own interpreter. When we start with philosophy, science, tradition, or our own culture as the context for understanding the Bible, we rob it of its fundamental authority, and impose upon it human authorities. Paul admonishes that we should rightly interpret the word of truth (2 Tim. 2:15) rather than handle it deceitfully (2 Cor. 4:2). Peter warns that if we twist the Scriptures, we do it to our own destruction (2 Peter 3:16). We are not to come to the Bible in human wisdom, but under the guidance of the Holy Spirit, comparing spiritual things with spiritual things (1 Cor. 2:12, 13).

The Second Coming and the Word of God

The authority of the Bible and the certainty of the Second Coming are closely linked, for our knowledge of the Second Coming depends upon the Bible. Many try to see the future totally apart from Scripture. Some seek information from spirits of the dead, from oracles such as the one at Delphi in Greece, from the reading of tarot cards or tea leaves. More "sophisticated" people tend to go to science and other human disciplines to try to predict the future. They examine data from natural events, economic laws, sociology, historical cycles of recurring events, human psychology, and other disciplines in their effort to foretell the future. Thus it is the goal of many in our contemporary era to discover the future without seeking any special word from the Lord.

Some wish to disregard the authority of the Bible when they develop their concept of the future. They attempt to make the future conform to their own dream of the ideal life, even if it means political and military revolution. For example, on its way to establishing the kingdom of God on earth, liberation theology analyzes the social and economic conditions of people and seeks to discover who is responsible for poverty. Once they believe they have achieved that, the liberation theologians or politicians then develop a plan to establish justice—to bring about, on their own, God's kingdom on earth. They even raise funds from global church agencies to provide weapons for revolutions in underprivileged countries. And in many other ways we find ourselves tempted to act independent of God in our efforts to control the future.

But without the Word of God our concepts of the future will be just as varied and flawed as the attempts to control it.

How can we know the future? God has revealed it to us! We

cannot gain knowledge of the Second Coming, for example, through philosophical speculation, science, or historical analysis. The human race can know that Christ is coming again only because of what He has revealed to us in His Word.

Still another connection exists between the Word of God and the Second Coming. Those who do not accept and follow the Word of God will fail to prepare for the coming of Christ. Paul mentions that those who do not believe the truth will follow the lawless one, who will entice them, not with the Word of God, but with his own power, signs, and deceptive wonders (2 Thess. 2:1-12). Because we stand in the presence of God and Jesus Christ, who will judge both the living and the dead at His appearing, we must preach the word. Unfortunately, some will not reject sound doctrine and will find themselves led astray by religious fables (2 Tim. 4:1-4). Peter echoes the same concern. If we do not follow the words spoken by the prophets and the apostles, we could fall under the influence of those who question the promise of the Second Coming. But we do not have to succumb to those who twist the Scriptures. His Word points us to new heavens and a new earth in which righteousness dwells (2 Peter 3:2-18).

Certainty of the Second Coming

We may rejoice that God has not left us in darkness regarding the future. The future does not lie in our hands, but rests in God's plans. And God has chosen to tell us about it. As Amos says: "Surely the Lord God does nothing, unless He reveals His secret to His servants the prophets" (Amos 3:7). The Bible makes a clear connection between the Second Coming and the Word of God. God inspired its writing that we might have hope (Rom. 15:4; cf. 1 Cor. 10:11). The Word of the Lord makes the promise of the Second Coming certain (1 Thess. 4:15). "Then he said to me, 'These words are faithful and true.' And the Lord God of the holy prophets sent His angel to show His servants the things which must shortly take place. 'Behold, I am coming quickly! Blessed is he who keeps the words of the prophecy of this book'" (Rev. 22:6-8). The security of the Second Coming rests in the certainty of the Bible, the Word of God. Peter exclaims that we have not followed cun-

THE CERTAINTY OF THE SECOND COMING

ningly devised fables. Instead, we have sure prophecy that came by divine intent rather than by human activity. If we follow it, it will lead us to the Second Coming (2 Peter 1:16-21).

The certainty of the Second Coming rests not in human genius, foresight, or control, but in the promises of the Word of God. Our confidence in the Second Advent therefore derives from the surety of the Bible, the Word of God. We trust the reliability of the Bible not on the basis of human genius, wisdom, insight, or knowledge, but in the power of God Himself. The certainty that the Bible is the Word of God is a result of faith, which is itself a gift from God (Eph. 2:8). Such faith is evidence of things beyond human sight (Heb. 1:11). We acquire it through the Word of God (Rom. 10:17).

How does the Word of God bring about faith? The Bible is the tool the Spirit uses to transform us (Eph. 6:17). Living and powerful, sharper than any two-edged sword (Heb. 4:12), it is capable of making its own way into any human heart open to God's message. That Word brought worlds into existence, sight to the blind, hearing to the deaf. When we read the Bible, it is as if God Himself were in the room speaking to us. It is not dead letters resting on the pages of a lifeless book, but is the living Word of God. Through His Word of truth God brings us to life (James 1:18). "Having been born again, not of corruptible seed but incorruptible, through the word of God which lives and abides forever" (1 Peter 1:23). Neither human intelligence nor human verification can bring us to faith (Luke 16:31). Only the Spirit of God creates a sense of conviction (Zech. 4:6; John 16:8; 1 Cor. 12:3). And the conviction that the Bible is the Word of God gives us certainty in our hope of the Second Coming.

In these last days, just before His return, God invites us to become part of the proclamation of the three angels' messages (Rev. 14). This will be our subject in chapter 9. He longs to have the Scripture fully preached, because He wants every person to have the opportunity to know Him as He is, the only true God. He knocks at the door of each heart, because He wants to come in and fellowship with us. Hold forth the Word of life, that you may rejoice in the day of the Lord! (Phil. 2:16).

Chapter 3

Creation and the Certainty of the Second Coming

WHO ARE WE? Are we the result of a rich prebiotic soup that formed from the concentration of chemicals in lakes and tidal pools? Did we evolve from there to self-replicating nucleic acids, and then to a primitive cell? Was our proud ancestry carried on by natural selection from the primitive cell, through primitive life forms to the more advanced forms of life, leading to the primates and finally the hominids? Are we here because the basic principle of the survival of the fittest guided our ancestry down to our generation? Are we explained and defined by the theory of evolution?

If so, what does that mean for who we are? Are we here by chance, because a lightning strike and a concentration of chemicals coincided billions of years ago? If that is the case, how should we then live? How should we relate to others? Does the principle of the survival of the fittest provide the foundation of our moral life? And if not, why not, and what would be morality's origin? If we are the culmination of long evolutionary development, does it mean that we depend solely on ourselves for our achievements, and that our mind provides the foundation of our knowledge? Are we therefore autonomous, independent of any force outside of ourselves, and thus the masters of our own personal universe? What does the future hold for the human race? Can we define salvation and heaven as the continuing progress of the evolutionary process?

Evolution and God

And if we are here because of evolutionary process, what does that say for God? Does He exist at all? If He does, who is

THE CERTAINTY OF THE SECOND COMING

He? Is He simply a principle we call chance? What kind of influence, if any, does He have on the universe? What role, if any, would He play in history, in our lives? Does He know that we exist? Does He even care? Is He some inanimate great force in the universe, or maybe a mastermind? Is He also a person? If He is a person, how does He relate to us?

Should He exist, did He initiate the first spark of life and then somehow guide the process of evolution (a hypothesis called theistic evolution)? If so, why did it take Him billions of years to bring evolution to the stage of human development? Is His problem one of limited power? Or is it that He really does not care? Why did He use the cruel process of the survival of the fittest to create humanity? Does that mean He is a tyrant? Or is He really a God of love doing the best that He can with His finite power? Perhaps He is a God of power and of love, but just not very smart—a little slow, but making it? And if He is a personal God, a God of love, why did it take Him so many millions and billions of years to get around to telling us about His love? Why did it require so long for Him to express it?

Could it be that God Himself is in a process of evolution? He was first of all a great power and got things going. Then He began to develop a mind, so that He could guide the process of evolution more skillfully. Next He evolved into a personal being, so that now, in the past several thousand years, He has desired to share Himself with His creation. If He is personal, how would we get to know Him so that we could enter a relationship with Him?

What implication does theistic evolution have for the way God acts in the world? If God either cannot or does not behave in the way that the Genesis creation account describes, then what does that say for other reports of His activities in the rest of the Bible? Did God bring about a worldwide flood and guide Noah's ark to safety? Did He really bring the children of Israel out of Egypt and through the Red Sea? Did He really come in Jesus Christ to become one among us, to die for our sins, to be resurrected on our behalf, and to ascend into heaven? Will He literally and visibly return to take us home with Himself? Will He create a new heaven and a new earth?

If we have a problem with the miracle of creation, why would we not also question the miracle of the resurrection, the Second Coming, and the creation of the new earth? And if we struggle with miracles, how do we account for the supposed evolution of the human race from the animal kingdom to our ability to think and make moral decisions? The infusion of mind and morality at some point in the history of evolution would be itself a miracle. Why not therefore accept the miracle of Creation recorded in Genesis?

Evolution, Sin, and Salvation

Suppose God did bring about life on our planet by the process of theistic evolution, developing it through the survival of the fittest from simple life forms to the complexity of a moral and intelligent creature called *Homo sapiens*. What would then be the meaning of sin and salvation? If humanity is in the process of evolutionary development, is sin simply a lack of progress? At what point did we become children of God? What role does Christ play? If we are only in some process of development, we would have no need of a substitute to die for us, since we did not fall from the image of God in the first place. One could hardly call our slow progress sin. Therefore, we do not need a Saviour. Is Christ then the peak of evolutionary development? Did He somehow become an example for us in order to speed up our development?

Evolution and the Bible

What would the theory of theistic evolution say for the nature of the Bible? In what sense, if any, would the Bible then be the Word of God? If the Bible is God's Word, and if His Word is the foundation of our life, including our understanding of the world, then on what basis would we reject the Creation account? Maybe the Bible is only the history of the evolution of human spirituality. Individuals and communities shared their religious concepts and passed them on from generation to generation. Spirituality matured through the process of evolution. Finally Jesus Christ Himself became the height of evolutionary spirituality. He is thereby the catalyst for the development of our own spirituality.

THE CERTAINTY OF THE SECOND COMING

As we can see, if we do not accept the biblical account of Creation, we are left with many questions, a few guesses, and no answers. We have only an uncertain identity. It puts the nature and even the existence of God into question. Our future is in limbo.

"Those who question the reliability of the Scripture records have let go their anchor and are left to beat about upon the rocks of infidelity. When they find themselves incapable of measuring the Creator and His works by their own imperfect knowledge of science, they question the existence of God and attribute infinite power to nature" (*Testimonies for the Church,* vol. 8, p. 258).

"God has permitted a flood of light to be poured upon the world in discoveries in science and art; but when professedly scientific men lecture and write upon these subjects from a merely human standpoint, they will assuredly come to wrong conclusions. The greatest minds, if not guided by the Word of God in their research, become bewildered in their attempts to investigate the relations of science and revelation. The Creator and His works are beyond their comprehension; and because they cannot explain these by natural laws, Bible history is considered unreliable. Those who doubt the reliability of the records of the Old and New Testaments will be led to go a step farther, and doubt the existence of God; and then, having let go their anchor, they are left to beat about upon the rocks of infidelity. Moses wrote under the guidance of the Spirit of God, and a correct theory of geology will never claim discoveries that cannot be reconciled with his statements" (*Lift Him Up,* p. 60).

The biblical concept of the origin of life and of the history of humanity is completely opposite from the evolutionary concept. The Bible declares that God created life and its habitable environment in six literal consecutive 24-hour days (Gen. 1). Exodus 20:11 and 31:17 confirm creation in six days. God gives the six-day creation as the reason for the fourth commandment. Instead of creating us during a period of billions of years, He "formed man of the dust of the ground, and breathed into his nostrils the breath of life; and man became a living being" (Gen. 2:7; cf. Mark 10:6).

While the theory of evolution envisions the formation of life during millions and billions of years, the Bible declares that Creation took place by the Word of God. "By the word of the Lord the heavens were made, and all the host of them by the breath of His mouth. . . . For He spoke, and it was done; he commanded, and it stood fast" (Ps. 33:6-9; cf. Ps. 148:5, 6; Isa. 45:12).

Some try to discount the historicity of Genesis 1-11 by saying that the chapters are not trying to relate what actually happened—they are poetry, not history. Their purpose consists of nothing more than conveying the message that in the beginning, God created. Thus the Bible does not give us the how of Creation, but merely the fact of Creation. However we view the question as to whether or not Genesis 1-11 is historical narrative or poetry really does not alter the outcome, for the Bible often uses poetry to present history. Thus the poetic argument does not really undermine the intended historicity of these chapters.

Scripture Confirms the Historicity of Genesis

In addition, we must allow Scripture to interpret itself. When we look at the whole of Scripture, we find that the Bible—including Christ Himself—took these chapters seriously as history. Paul confirms that "Adam [not some bit of slime in the water] was formed first, then Eve" (1 Tim. 2:13; cf. Luke 3:38; Rom. 5:14; 1 Cor. 15:22, 45). Christ referred to the creation of the first couple: "Have you not read that He who made them at the beginning 'made them male and female'" (Matt. 19:4). The Saviour uses this fact as a ground for morality based upon the design of God: "For this reason a man shall leave his father and mother and be joined to his wife, and the two shall become one flesh" (verse 5). Morality rests upon God's original plan for humanity when He created them in Eden, not upon a theory of survival of the fittest. Also, Christ took seriously the Genesis story of Noah and the Flood: "For as in the days before the flood, they were eating and drinking, marrying and giving in marriage, until the day that Noah entered the ark, and did not know until the flood came and took them all away" (Matt. 24:38, 39; cf. 2 Peter 2:5).

The agent in Creation, according to the Bible, was not evolution driven by the survival of the fittest, but rather God's Son,

THE CERTAINTY OF THE SECOND COMING

Jesus Christ Himself. "In the beginning was the Word, and the Word was with God, and the Word was God. He was in the beginning with God. All things were made through Him, and without Him nothing was made that was made" (John 1:1-3; cf. verse 10). "By him were all things created that are in heaven and that are on earth, visible and invisible. . . . And in Him all things consist" (Col. 1:16, 17; cf. 1 Cor. 8:6; Eph. 3:9; Heb. 1:1, 2).

Our concept of Creation also affects our understanding of God and of how we relate to Him. The fact that God is Creator provides the foundation of our respect (Isa. 17:7, 8) and our worship of Him: "For thus says the Lord, who created the heavens, who is God, who formed the earth and made it, who has established it, who did not create it in vain, who formed it to be inhabited: 'I am the Lord, and there is no other'" (Isa. 45:18). "You are worthy, O Lord, to receive glory and honor and power; for You created all things, and by Your will they exist and were created" (Rev. 4:11; cf. Neh. 9:6; Acts 14:15; 1 Cor. 8:6). Creation distinguishes God from other deities (1 Chron. 16:26).

In addition, it forms the basis of our relationship with Him, for in the beginning He made us for fellowship (Eph. 3:9). He who first commanded light to beam out of darkness also shines into our hearts the light of the knowledge of God's glory revealed through Jesus Christ (2 Cor. 4:6). By virtue of His creative power, He is the basis of our own strength (Ps. 121:2; 124:8). Our acceptance of the account of Creation rests upon faith: "By faith we understand that the worlds were framed by the word of God, so that the things which are seen were not made of things which are visible" (Heb. 11:3).

The biblical account of humanity differs greatly from that offered by evolution. We are not sons and daughters of primates, but sons and daughters of God! Adam's genealogy does not trace back to a primitive cell. He was the son of God (Luke 3:38). We are not created in the image of some beast, but the image and likeness of God Himself (Gen. 1:26-28; 5:1, 2).

"The conclusions which learned men have reached as the result of their scientific investigations are carefully taught and fully explained; while the impression is distinctly given that if these learned men are correct, the Bible cannot be. These philosophers would make us believe that man, the crowning work of creation, came by slow degrees from the savage state, and that farther back, he was evolved from the race of brutes. They are so intent upon excluding God from the sovereignty of the universe, that they demean man, and defraud him of the dignity of his origin. Nature is exalted above the God of nature; she is idolized, while her Creator is buried up and concealed from sight by science falsely so-called" (*Signs of the Times,* Mar. 20, 1884).

Creation and the Second Coming

The Bible links the historical accounts of Creation and the Flood and the Second Coming. "Scoffers will come in the last days, walking according to their own lusts, and saying, 'Where is the promise of His coming? For since the fathers fell asleep, all things continue as they were from the beginning of creation.' For this they willfully forget: that by the word of God the heavens were of old, and the earth standing out of water and in the water, by which the world that then existed perished, being flooded with water. But the heavens and the earth which are now preserved by the same word, are reserved for fire until the day of judgment and perdition of ungodly men" (2 Peter 3:3-7). Christ made that same connection: "But as the days of Noah were, so also will the coming of the Son of Man be. For as in the days before the flood, they were eating and drinking, marrying and giving in marriage, until the day that Noah entered the ark, and did not know until the flood came and took them all away, so also will the coming of the Son of Man be" (Matt. 24:37-39). Thus Scripture uses the historical conditions of humanity at the time of Noah as an analogy to the times just before the coming of Christ. Furthermore, the same word that brought about Creation and the Flood will bring about the destruction at the Second Coming.

Theistic evolution finds it necessary to reinterpret the biblical concept of the Second Coming and the new earth. If God did not break into history in Creation, then surely He will not do so in a literal, visible Second Coming. Nor, if He does not create by the word of His mouth, will He re-create in the resurrection. And if

He did not originally create the Garden of Eden, will He re-create the new earth? For the theistic evolutionist, eschatology is not a decisive entrance of God into history at the Second Coming. It is the continuing evolution of a better life, a process that humanity accelerates by bringing about a moral and just society through such activities as revolt, rebellion, redistribution of wealth, education, etc. Thank God, though, we can have hope in the future Second Coming because God is our Creator and Redeemer!

Adventism will not be Adventism if it accepts theistic evolution. The active God who created by the word of His mouth, who communicated through the prophets, who lived among us, died in our place, was resurrected, and ascended to minister for us, who will return the second time to take us home with Himself, who will bring about the resurrection of the dead and the re-creation of the new earth, and who will finally destroy sin—we cannot worship such a God if He does not exist. Adventists do not worship a god who dragged his creatures through the slime of evolution, but the God of Creation, a personal God who desires to fellowship with us and to dwell among us. We worship Him because He created us. It is that act that distinguishes Him from would-be gods.

We have seen in chapter 1 that Christianity is a relationship with God and Jesus Christ. It is not an imaginary, contentless relationship, but one based upon knowledge of the "only true God" (John 17:3). If our relationship is with any other deity, it is idolatry. Whether in its Darwinian form that rejects the existence of God, or in its theistic manifestation that claims God as the controller of the evolutionary process, the theory of evolution denies the biblical doctrine of God. It builds another concept of divinity based upon science, history, and philosophy that denies the God who has revealed Himself. Relying upon human ability to discover "truth," such approaches follow the same path Satan did. They set us up as independent of God, capable ourselves of defining or creating a god out of our own imagination.

Evolutionary theory requires that we rewrite the history of God, and therefore redefine His nature. In so doing, it leads us to enter a relationship with a false god, an idol. When Christ appears the second time, He desires to return to a people who are waiting for Him, not for some other false god. He will come to a people who are like Him in character, not like our "designer gods" that are the creation of our own imagination. Christ wants a people who are not in the dark about who He is. Therefore, He is calling forth a people who will accept and proclaim the fullness of the biblical message—the everlasting gospel—part of which is "worship Him who made heaven and earth, the sea and springs of water" (Rev. 14:7).

Chapter 4

BY ROLAND R. HEGSTAD

Of Relative Truths and Redemptive Symbols

AS THE SCRUFFY youth sauntered along the boardwalk in Santa Monica, California, I saw it on the seat of his worn and torn pair of Levi shorts. The American flag. Old Glory. I didn't stand at attention, didn't salute it. If I'd had a paddle (and a smidgen more courage), I'd have whacked his star-spangled rear.

In most countries the authorities would happily have jailed the youth for misusing the flag. But not in the United States, where the Supreme Court has said that the First Amendment's guarantee of free speech protects the desecration of the flag. A few years ago Congress, too, took a similar stance. Not that the legislators were unanimous. The speaker of the House didn't think the Constitution should be used to protect "the sparse and scattered and despicable conduct of a few who would dishonor the flag or belittle it."

Another congressman, calling the flag a "unique symbol," said it should not be desecrated, because "too many people have paid for it with their blood. Too many have marched behind it. Too many have slept in a box under it. Too many kids and parents and widows have accepted this [symbol] as the last remembrance of their most precious son. Too many to have this [flag] ever demeaned."

A flag is the symbol of a nation. When we salute the flag we pledge our loyalty to our homeland. Should someone attack it, we rush to its defense. Small wonder we feel offended when we see our flag adorning someone's jean-clad posterior. Or decorating a garbage can. Or burned for one cause or another at a protest rally.

And yet a flag is essentially a piece of cloth. Were I to put a match to a piece of blue cloth, a piece of white cloth, and a piece

OF RELATIVE TRUTHS AND REDEMPTIVE SYMBOLS

of red cloth, no American, however loyal, would protest. But put them together, link them with stars, and the pieces of material become something more than the sum of their parts. They turn into the symbol of our country.

A day, too, may be something more than the sum of its parts—the seconds, the minutes, and the hours that comprise it. Birthdays, anniversaries, graduation—they are more than just another day. How much more true of the Sabbath—a unit of time cut from the fabric of eternity itself and given to earthlings by their Creator. When as children of God we weekly salute this symbol of our heavenly homeland, we acknowledge God's creative authority over the embassy of our heart.

Over this symbol as over the flag a controversy rages, one with roots in centuries of history. Adding international currency to the issue is the recent papal encyclical *Dies Domini*. Abandoning the centuries-old claim that the Roman Catholic Church has changed even the law of God, it attempts a biblical defense for the Christian Sunday.

For several reasons Seventh-day Adventists can be thankful for *Dies Domini*. First, it focuses the world's attention on God's symbol of His creative and re-creative powers. Second, it directs Christians of whatever profession to the Bible for a discussion of the issues. And the Christian who comes to the Bible seeking truth about God's Sabbath will soon determine that Pope John Paul's day of worship is 24 hours off, and that far more than a matter of hours is at stake. The Bible reveals the seventh-day Sabbath to be (1) a symbol of God's authority, (2) a test of our loyalty, (3) the definer of who and how we are to worship, and (4) God's redemptive assurance that "all things bright and beautiful" shall soon again be ours.

1. The Sabbath as a Symbol of God's Authority

Uncle Oscar Hegstad, a short bank teller-like person with frameless glasses and a small but determined chin, was the first Seventh-day Adventist in our family. My father's oldest brother, he attended an Adventist tent meeting in Devils Lake, North Dakota, many decades ago. Night after night my Lutheran uncle

THE CERTAINTY OF THE SECOND COMING

came home angry, but with every text written down. And night after night he studied them and prayed over them. When the meetings ended, Oscar was a Seventh-day Adventist, a status that for years made him, in the family's estimation, the only nut on the family tree.

During my grade school years in Wauna, Oregon, he was a colporteur. When he'd stop by our home and talk with us about his religious convictions, he was persuasive. I used to love bacon and eggs for breakfast, but after he got done telling me how filthy pork was, I dropped it—in all its permutations—for life.

But the Sabbath was another matter. Uncle Oscar could summon science to his side against pork, but not on behalf of the seventh-day Sabbath, which just didn't seem to make sense. First, it seemed as if only a few religious oddballs observed it. Second, it appeared irrational. Most of the other commandments made sense: anybody—Christian or Muslim or Buddhist or atheist—knew that they shouldn't steal, lie, kill. If the Lord had said, "Rest on one day in seven," that would have made sense, because everybody needs rest. And the word "Sabbath" itself means rest. But the Sabbath commandment—arbitrarily, I thought—specified cessation from work on the *seventh* day:

"Remember the Sabbath day, to keep it holy. Six days you shall labor and do all your work, but the seventh day is the Sabbath of the Lord your God. In it you shall do no work: you, nor your son, nor your daughter, nor your male servant, nor your female servant, nor your cattle, nor your stranger who is within your gates. For in six days the Lord made the heavens and the earth, the sea, and all that is in them, and rested the seventh day. Therefore the Lord blessed the Sabbath day and hallowed it" (Ex. 20:8-11). As Uncle Oscar pointed out, *hallowed* means "set apart for holy use"—a definition that seems to have eluded the writer of the recent encyclical.

Of course, the Sabbath is only the fourth of the Ten Commandments. In their universal format—"You shall love the Lord your God with all your heart, with all your soul, and with all your mind. . . . You shall love your neighbor as yourself" (Matt. 22:37-39)—they are a universal "Bill of Rights" pointing

OF RELATIVE TRUTHS AND REDEMPTIVE SYMBOLS

the way to eternal happiness. The apostle James calls the Ten Commandments the "law of liberty" (James 2:12). Though I was raised with a wholesome disrespect for all institutional religion and an abiding dislike for ministers, I don't recall that either my parents or I had much trouble with the idea that God's got a law—assuming, of course, that He exists. It did seem logical that rulers would have legislation to govern their subjects.

Uncle Oscar observed that the Sabbath commandment, alone among the ten, identifies God as Creator and asserts His authority because of His creative act. The Sabbath is like a king's seal, Uncle Oscar explained. The Creator uses it as the stamp of His authority. "I made you," He says, "and I know what is best for you." And "you," said Uncle Oscar, doesn't mean just the Jew. The Sabbath, Jesus told us, "was made for man" (Mark 2:27). The first Jew came along millennia after humanity's creation. Almost every Christian, Oscar argued, will tell you that a Christian cannot, in good conscience, violate nine of the Ten Commandments. The exception, of course, is the fourth.

So important are the principles of God's law that Jesus died for our disobeying them (see Rom. 3:23 and 6:23). The good news—the "gospel"—is that Jesus let human beings execute Him to spare us the death penalty. One cannot, therefore, separate the Ten Commandments and the gospel. If God could have done away with the law, Jesus would not have had to die. But if we dispensed with the gospel, all the world would perish. So both gospel and law offer reasons to acknowledge God's authority as Creator and as Redeemer.

2. The Sabbath as a Test of Loyalty

Uncle Oscar argued that if one accepts the premise that God, as Creator, has the right to instruct His creation how to live happily, then one should accept the corollary—it is His children's loving obligation to fly the flag of their loyalty, the Sabbath, over the embassy of their heart.

In fact, Jesus made observance of all His commandments a love test: "If you love Me," He told His disciples, "keep My commandments" (John 14:15). He presented it as a test of friendship: "Ye are My friends if you do whatever I command you" (John 15:14). And He emphatically linked obedience with true worship, saying that it is of no use for religious leaders to worship Him because they teach human-made commandments as though they were God's rules (Mark 7:7, 8).

You'll not find such explicit warnings in the encyclical's passionate plea to Catholics to keep Sunday holy. And surely Adventists will not be the only sincere Christians who will note the omission.

How does the Sabbath become a test of God's authority and our loyalty? I remember Uncle Oscar referring to Daniel 7:25, which speaks of a power that would arise and "think to change times and laws" (KJV).

If I'd had a part in such a challenge to God's authority, I surely wouldn't want to admit it. But the incredible fact is that church spokespersons, both Protestant and Catholic, admit that no Bible warrant exists for discarding the Sabbath for Sunday. And on the basics, they agree how it did happen.

Here's one explanation, typical of many from Catholic sources: "Nowhere in the Bible do we find that Christ or the apostles ordered that the Sabbath be changed from Saturday to Sunday. We have the commandment of God . . . to keep holy the Sabbath day, that is the seventh day of the week, Saturday. Today most Christians keep Sunday because it has been revealed to us by the [Roman Catholic] church outside the Bible" (*Catholic Virginian,* Oct. 3, 1947). Other Catholic sources, including catechisms, chide Protestants for accepting a change made by the church while claiming to go strictly by Scripture.

Peter Heylyn, an Episcopal historian, observed, "Take which you will, either the Fathers or the moderns, and we shall find no Lord's day instituted by any apostolical mandate, no Sabbath set on foot by them upon the first day of the week" (*History of the Sabbath,* p. 410).

Johann Neander wrote that "the festival of Sunday, like all other festivals, was always only a human ordinance" (*The History of the Christian Religion and Church*).

And now the pope, likely for reasons of ecumenism, has

OF RELATIVE TRUTHS AND REDEMPTIVE SYMBOLS

changed the party line, arguing that the Bible reveals that it is God Himself who shifted the Sabbath to Sunday! But Jesus said: "You lay aside the commandments of God so you can follow your own traditions." Hopefully some Protestants will not forget why "protest" is part of their name.

How did the change come about?

First, Jewish revolts against the Romans during the first and second centuries made being Jewish perilous. Because the early Christians kept the Sabbath, the Romans regarded them as just another Jewish sect. Worshiping on the "venerable day of the sun" was much safer than worshiping with the Jews on Sabbath.

Then, after the apostles and their followers died, church leaders substituted a new day for worship in place of the Sabbath. The change took place gradually, perhaps beginning with a yearly commemoration of Jesus' resurrection. With the encouragement of the bishop of Rome, Sunday became a weekly celebration.

In the fourth century, along came the Roman emperor Constantine, an astute politician who (1) supported Christianity, (2) decreed that pagan and Christian alike worship on Sunday, and (3) enacted the world's first civil Sunday law. The emerging Papacy eventually, through an alliance with the state, persecuted those followers of Jesus who, in regard to Sabbath observance and other biblical practices, insisted on giving loyalty to the Creator instead of His creatures.

This much is conclusive: First, that the seventh day is the Sabbath. Second, that worship on Sunday developed as the church slid into apostasy. Third, that the Bible nowhere authorizes the change to Sunday. In fact, the issue in the New Testament never deals with *which* day is the Sabbath, but rather with *how* we should observe it. And that issue, as Seventh-day Adventists well know, is not dead. . . .

3. The Sabbath Defines Not Only Who Is to Be Worshiped, but How

Scripture reveals—and Uncle Oscar would turn to the verses—that it has ever been Lucifer's ambition to mount the throne of God and usurp the worship due only to Him. "You have said in your heart: 'I will ascend into heaven; I will exalt my throne above the stars of God; . . . I will be like the Most High'" (Isa. 14:13, 14).

The controversy that rent the fabric of heaven itself began with Lucifer's passion to receive worship. And it continued on earth as heaven cast the rebel leader out with his seduced legions. The Bible reveals a critical skirmish on a wilderness battlefield, when Lucifer, masquerading as an agent of God, confronts Jesus with three temptations. Transparent in the account is the rebel's continued determination to obtain worship.

"The devil took him [Jesus] to a very high mountain, and from there showed him all the kingdoms of the world and their magnificence. 'Everything there I will give you,' he said to him, 'if you will fall down and worship me.'" Jesus answered Satan's temptations with the Word of God: "'Away with you, Satan!' replied Jesus. The scripture says, 'Thou shalt worship the Lord thy God and him only shalt thou serve.' Then the devil left him" (Matt. 4:8-11, Phillips).

Not left on the battlefield, however, was the devil's craving for worship. He departed still determined to secure from the church the worship that he could not get from its Founder in the wilderness. We're indebted to John the revelator for an intelligence report on where Satan went from his defeat at the hands of Christ. Chapter 12 pictures Satan making war plans (Rev. 12:17) against those who, in the end-time, shall persist in loyally keeping the commandments of God and thus bear witness to their Saviour's creative and re-creative acts.

Satan focuses his fury particularly on the Sabbath commandment, because above all others it frustrates his ambition to usurp the authority of God's Word and to be worshiped. In Revelation 13 John reveals the devil's strategy against the church. In every confrontation—verses 4, 8, 12, 15—the issue is authority and worship. By deceit, persecution, wonders, signs, miracles, Satan attempts to gain the adoration of all humanity. And in a final desperate gambit, just as he appeared to Christ in the wilderness as an angel from heaven, he shall in the end-time present himself to humanity as the Messiah!

OF RELATIVE TRUTHS AND REDEMPTIVE SYMBOLS

In Revelation 14 John commissions Christ's last legion to counter the devil, not with miracles, but with God's Word. Foremost is the preaching of the everlasting gospel to "those who dwell on the earth—to every nation, tribe, tongue, and people" (Rev. 14:6). The message is urgent because, as John reveals, the hour of God's judgment has come.

In response, God's loyal followers "reverence" Him and "give glory to him" (Phillips) by inviting Him to reveal Himself to the world through them! And they, in turn, call the world to "worship Him who made heaven and earth, and the sea and springs of water" (verse 7). Where do those words appear elsewhere in the Bible? *In the Sabbath commandment!* What is the issue? *Allegiance to God's Word and worship. The world must be in terrible danger of worshiping a counterfeit god on his counterfeit day. To pay homage to their designer gods rather than to the God of the Bible.* Once again, at world's end, the paramount issue in the great controversy between Christ and Satan shall be that of the authority of God's Word and who is to be worshiped. And the mark of discipleship shall be observance of the Sabbath—*God's* Sabbath, the seventh day of the week!

As these truths confronted me during my first year of college, I faced a choice—just as Uncle Oscar had, just as millions throughout the centuries have, and just as millions more shall: Either to join a people who "keep the commandments of God and have the testimony of Jesus Christ" (Rev. 12:17), or to side with those who claim that the church rather than Scripture defines God's will.

I should not ignore those Christians who faithfully observe Sunday in honor of Christ's resurrection, however. Let me pause a gentle moment to comment on their case. Unfortunately for the resurrection hypothesis, no scripture transfers God's seal of authority to Sunday. Instead, Jesus warned emphatically against attempting to change His commandments. Note Matthew 5:17-20: "You must not think that I have come to abolish the Law or the Prophets; I have not come to abolish them but to complete them. Indeed, I assure you that, while Heaven and earth last, the Law will not lose a single dot or comma until its purpose is complete. This means that whoever now relaxes one of the least of these commandments and teaches men to do the same will himself be called least in the kingdom of Heaven. But whoever teaches and practices them will be called great in the kingdom of Heaven" (Phillips).

No, I don't agree with those who keep Sunday because Jesus was resurrected on that day. The New Testament gives us another ordinance by which we celebrate Christ's death, burial, and resurrection. Called baptism, you can read about it in Romans 6. Through baptism, Paul tells us, we figuratively go down into the grave with Jesus and come up as participants in His resurrection.

While those who commemorate the Resurrection by Sunday worship may be wrong, one must say two things in their behalf: 1. They do make more sense than those who argue that Sunday observance has its roots in the fourth commandment. 2. Many Sundaykeeping Christians trust fully in Christ for their salvation. They keep the wrong day for the right reason. And what of Seventh-day Sabbath observers who believe their Sabbathkeeping will save them? They honor the right day for the wrong reason.

Faced with such biblical evidences, I was baptized at the end of my first year of college. My decision involved acknowledging the authority of God's Word and His right to my allegiance. "When I stand in judgment before my Creator," I asked myself, "which argument would I rather advance in my defense: The church said, or the Bible said?"

However, meaningful Sabbath observance encompasses much more than just the "facts" of the Sabbath. We have altogether too many members in the church who know everything I've said to be true, but who are not really Sabbathkeepers. To truly rest on the Sabbath day involves more than knowing Saturday is the Sabbath. That the Sabbath is a symbol of God's authority, and further, the test of our loyalty.

One can believe all this and still be lost. Our right to the kingdom depends today on what it always has—perfect obedience to God's will. And we are no more capable of producing that today than we've ever been, "for all have sinned and fall short of the glory of God" (Rom. 3:23). Salvation is the "free

OF RELATIVE TRUTHS AND REDEMPTIVE SYMBOLS

gift" of "eternal life through Jesus Christ our Lord" (Rom. 6:23, Phillips). When Jesus invites us to rest, or "Sabbath," with Him, He requests that we not only cease from our physical labors, but rest trustfully in His finished work of redemption.

4. So I Keep the Sabbath Because It Is Christ's Redemptive Assurance That "All Things Bright and Beautiful" Shall Soon Again Be Ours

Let me tell you about my aunt Sylvia Peterson, a perpetually pleasant person who, with her husband, Stanley, lived on Puget Island, in the Columbia, some 28 miles east of Astoria, Oregon. My high school sweetheart and I used to stop at their home on our way to dances in the old Norse Hall. Never did Aunt Sylvia get on my case. Instead, she served up warm molasses bread and fruit salad shot through with whipped cream and walnuts. And it was she I listened to when, after Grandma Hegstad's death during my senior year of high school, I asked whether there was indeed a God and what happens when one dies. I remember Aunt Sylvia for two graces: (1) her assurance of redemption and (2) her kindness to everyone.

My aunt knew who she was—a daughter of the King. She loved Jesus for taking her sins to Calvary, where she should have hung, and stamping her account "Paid in full!" Aunt Sylvia treasured His assurance that "no one can snatch them [His children] out of my hand" (John 10:28, Phillips). Every Sabbath reminded her that God's work on her behalf was finished on the sixth day (Luke 23:54), just as Creation was (Gen. 2:1-3). So every Sabbath she rested in the assurance of both a finished creation and a finished redemption.

From Aunt Sylvia I learned that only when one sees the Sabbath in the context of the gospel, only when one thrills to the assurance of a finished work at Calvary, can one truly worship on the Sabbath. It was this understanding of the Sabbath that sent her out on missions of mercy as a gracious witness for her Saviour. To her, the essence of Sabbathkeeping was people to love rather than rules to obey (see Luke 13:12-16).

Come with me, then, to Puget Island for a brief remembrance of her works of mercy. The Peterson home was open to all. She and Stanley used to take in problem children that the state social agencies couldn't help. They loved them, worked them on the farm, and in several instances educated them along with their three daughters. Sylvia was the Dorcas leader of the little Seventh-day Adventist church just across the bridge in Cathlamet, Washington. If anyone for 20 miles up and down the Columbia was sick, Aunt Sylvia was there with a hot meal, a good book, or even a vacuum cleaner. In her Sabbath ministry—and it extended to the six other days as well—Aunt Sylvia was fulfilling the mission of Jesus, as forecast by the gospel prophet Isaiah: "To loose the bonds of wickedness, to undo the heavy burdens, to let the oppressed go free, and . . . [to] break every yoke . . . to share your bread with the hungry, and that you bring to your house the poor who are cast out; when you see the naked, that you cover him, and hide not yourself from your own flesh" (Isa. 58:6, 7).

That, she taught me, was the way you bring "Sabbath" to people. As Christ's ministry documents, deeds of mercy and healing and kindness and the Sabbath go together, because, since the Fall, the Sabbath speaks to us of restoration. It's why Jesus performed many of His restorative miracles on the Sabbath. And it's why Aunt Sylvia spent her Sabbaths wiping tears and sweeping sadness right out the door.

When she died in her 60s of a heart attack, most of Puget Island and Cathlamet, population 635, came to the funeral, along with people from up and down both the Oregon and Washington sides of the Columbia. Unable to all get into the little church, they filled the lawn and looked and listened through the church windows. They all loved Aunt Sylvia, and when they thought of her, they were celebrating what God has ever intended the Sabbath to be.

Both Aunt Sylvia and Uncle Oscar contributed to my decision to commit my life to Christ and to ministry in a church that treasures the commandments of God and the faith of Jesus. I plan to visit both of them in that land where "all things bright and beautiful" shall be ours again.

OF RELATIVE TRUTHS AND REDEMPTIVE SYMBOLS

"For as the new heavens and the new earth, which I will make, shall remain before me, saith the Lord, so shall your seed and your name remain. And it shall come to pass, from one new moon to another, and from one Sabbath to another, shall all flesh come to worship before me, saith the Lord" (Isa. 66:22, 23, KJV).

When I meet Uncle Oscar someday soon after Christ returns, I'll probably say to him, "I learned a few things about the Sabbath along the way, things you didn't teach me. Things I had to learn from Aunt Sylvia." And he'll probably respond, "Roland, so did I." And I'll ask both of them, "What made you determine to honor the Sabbath?" And they'll probably answer: "We honored the Sabbath as a symbol of God's authority, as the test of loyalty, and as the definer of who was to be worshiped and how. Each Sabbath we worshiped because of its invitation to know God as our Creator and Sustainer. We honored it because of its assurance of Christ's perfect and finished redemptive work, and because it pointed us to the restoration of all things bright and beautiful. The Sabbath brought us to God as our personal friend who desired to spend time with us. We fell in love with God by worshiping Him on His holy day, and we therefore responded by pledging Him our allegiance.

"We found the Sabbath to be a unique symbol. And we decided that too many people have paid for it with their blood, too many have accepted the symbol in remembrance of their Saviour—too many to have it ever demeaned."

If you're comfortable with the Sabbath as Uncle Oscar and Aunt Sylvia understood it and lived it, I'd be comfortable in inviting you to join the Lord of the Sabbath in Sabbath services from week to week. And I'd like to put you down for an appointment with family and friends in the new heavens and the new earth, where your seed and your name shall remain forever.

Chapter 5

The First Coming Prepares for the Second Coming

GLORY TO GOD in the highest, and on earth peace, good will toward men!" (Luke 2:14). "I bring you good tidings of great joy. . . . For there is born to you this day in the city of David a Savior, who is Christ the Lord" (verses 10, 11).

Ho-hum! We have heard these words a thousand times—old news from 2,000 years ago. Sure, we recall the incident every year at Christmas when we receive gifts, take a few days off from the job, and visit relatives. But basically, the story has been told too many times to be relevant anymore.

Stop a moment, though! Suppose the Son of God had not become the Son of man. What if the infinite God had not made the infinite sacrifice to become one with us? Imagine that Jesus had not entered this world as a baby to live as we must and to die on our behalf. What if He had not died in our place or been resurrected for us? Where would we be today? Even more important, who would we be today? What would be our self-concept if we had no knowledge of God, no hope of the resurrection, no certainty of the Second Coming, and no concept of life eternal in fellowship with God?

Instead of being stale history, the First Advent is rather the very lifeblood of our existence. It is the event of the ages that makes life worth living—that gives it meaning, purpose, and hope. The Christmas story portrays the mystery of mysteries and the wonder of wonders that the Son of God, the Creator of the universe, would leave heaven and the fellowship of His Father to become the Saviour of the world!

Fully God, Fully Human

Who was Jesus? Why has His life made such a difference for

THE FIRST COMING PREPARES FOR . . .

us? First of all, Jesus was fully God. "In Him dwells all the fullness of the Godhead bodily" (Col. 2:9; cf. Phil. 2:6). Isaiah foretold that Jesus would be the mighty God, the everlasting Father (Isa. 9:6). In his Gospel, John emphasized that "in the beginning was the Word, and the Word was with God, and the Word was God. He was in the beginning with God. All things were made through Him, and without Him nothing was made that was made" (John 1:1-3; cf. John 8:58). Because He was God, He had life inherently within Himself (John 1:4; 5:21-26).

But Jesus was also fully human. Isaiah prophesied that He would not overwhelm the human race through physical attractiveness, power, or similar traits (Isa. 53:2). He entered our world through human birth (Gal. 4:4; Isa. 7:14). Made flesh, He dwelt among us (John 1:14). As a human being, He humbled Himself, not only to the level of a servant, but finally to the point of death (Phil. 2:7, 8). Indeed, it is a great mystery that God should manifest Himself in human flesh (1 Tim. 3:16). Christ did not "make believe" that He had human nature, but really took it. "'As the children are partakers of flesh and blood, he also himself likewise took part of the same.' He was the son of Mary; He was of the seed of David according to human descent" (*Review and Herald,* Apr. 5, 1906). "For our sake Jesus emptied Himself of His glory; He clothed His divinity with humanity that He might touch humanity, that His personal presence might be among us, that we might know that He was acquainted with all our trials, and sympathized with our grief, that every son and daughter of Adam might understand that Jesus is the friend of sinners" (*Signs of the Times,* Apr. 18, 1892).

The first coming of Christ reestablished the face-to-face communication with God that humanity had lost in Eden. As the God-man, Christ came as the revelation of the Father (John 1:18). "He who has seen Me has seen the Father" (John 14:9; cf. Matt. 11:27). "Christ alone was able to represent the Deity. He who had been in the presence of the Father from the beginning, He who was the express image of the invisible God, was alone sufficient to accomplish this work. No verbal description could reveal God to the world. Through a life of purity, a life of perfect trust and submission to the will of God, a life of humiliation such as even the highest seraph in heaven would have shrunk from, God Himself must be revealed to humanity. In order to do this, our Saviour clothed His divinity with humanity. He employed the human faculties, for only by adopting these could He be comprehended by humanity. Only humanity could reach humanity. He lived out the character of God through the human body which God had prepared for Him. He blessed the world by living out in human flesh the life of God, thus showing that He had the power to unite humanity to divinity" (*Review and Herald,* June 25, 1895).

The humanity of Christ meant that He faced the same temptations that all humanity struggles with. He can sympathize with us, for He was tempted in all points as we are! (Heb. 4:15; 2:18). Christ placed Himself in Adam's position to gain victory where humanity had failed. Some might argue that temptation could not really have overcome Christ, that unlike us there was no possibility of His yielding to the tempter. But that would have made a mockery of His condescending to become one with us. Christ did not come to play a game, but really to put human nature upon Himself. "Our Saviour took humanity, with all its liabilities. He took the nature of man, with the possibility of yielding to temptation. We have nothing to bear which He has not endured" (*The Desire of Ages,* p. 117). "Could Satan in the least particular have tempted Christ to sin, he would have bruised the Saviour's head. As it was, he could only touch His heel. Had the head of Christ been touched, the hope of the human race would have perished. Divine wrath would have come upon Christ as it came upon Adam. Christ and the church would have been without hope" (*Selected Messages,* book 1, p. 256).

Parallel Temptations

The temptation of Christ in the wilderness paralleled that of Adam and Eve in the garden. Satan approached Adam and Eve on their willingness to rely upon the Word of God alone in their decision as to how to relate to the tree in the center of the garden. Unfortunately, they did not choose to let the Word guide them. The fallen angel questioned what the Creator had already declared: "Has God indeed said?" (Gen. 3:1). "Is it really true that you will die if you eat of the fruit? Look at what your senses tell you. The serpent has eaten of the fruit and now has the ability to speak! If you perform the same scientific experiment, your powers will increase also—you will become as gods and will never die! Furthermore," the tempter continued, "a God of love would not destroy a creature whom He has created. Philosophy tells us that would be contrary to reason. Therefore, it is all right to ignore the Word of God and eat the fruit."

"Christ, in the wilderness of temptation, stood in Adam's place to bear the test he failed to endure" (*The Seventh-day Adventist Bible Commentary,* Ellen G. White Comments, vol. 5, p. 1081; cf. *The Desire of Ages,* p. 118). The setting for Christ's temptation was His baptism. The voice of God had spoken at the baptism, saying: "This is My beloved Son, in whom I am well pleased" (Matt. 3:17). Satan, witnessing that event, understood that God through Christ was reestablishing direct contact with the human race. The most intense hatred toward Christ arose in his heart. The Father's majestic voice, affirming Jesus as His Son, sounded to Satan like a death knell. Immediately he determined to break the contact between heaven and earth by tempting Jesus to sin (*The Seventh-day Adventist Bible Commentary,* Ellen G. White Comments, vol. 5, p. 1078).

God permitted Satan that opportunity. Jesus went into the wilderness and fasted for 40 days. When Christ was weak and emaciated from hunger, the devil came to Him with the same temptation he had used in Eden, that of casting doubt on the Word of God. At Christ's baptism God declared Jesus to be His Son. Now Satan challenged: "If You are the Son of God" (Matt. 4:3). Christ had the same options open to Him as had been available to Adam and Eve. He could have answered, "Why yes, I will give you scientific proof of My Sonship. I will turn these stones into bread." Or He could have questioned His Sonship from a philosophical standpoint—"A God of love would not allow His Son to be alone in the wilderness without food and companionship, subject to the wild beasts of the desert." Instead Christ firmly answered each of Satan's three challenges, "It is written!" (Matt. 4:4, 7, 10). The temptation Christ faced was to take Himself out of His Father's hands, thus distrusting God's goodness and disbelieving His Word and authority. Satan sought to lure Him into living independently, autonomously, from His Father and to work a miracle on His own behalf. The devil tried to trick Christ into proving His divinity on His own. But Jesus triumphed through relying upon the Word of God alone. A "thus said the Lord" was more powerful than any miracle or evidence appealing to the senses. It was above all human needs—"I don't have to have bread, but I must live by the Word of God!"

Intensity of Christ's Temptations

Christ faced temptations greater than any human has ever endured. None of us have struggled with the possibility of saving ourselves by employing our own divinity. During His ministry He could have silenced the questions and the jeers of the rulers by a simple manifestation of His divinity. In Gethsemane He could have summoned throngs of angels to protect Himself. When standing accused before the high priest He could have used His divine power to lay His enemies in the dust (*The Desire of Ages,* p. 700). And He could have avoided humiliation, shame, and death by coming down from the cross.

Not only were the temptations of Christ more intense than ours; He also met them at the depth of human weakness. He faced temptation in the wilderness after 40 days of starvation. On the cross He overcame at His weakest moment, having endured the weight of the sins of the world as well as sleeplessness, hunger, torture, and the physical agony of the cross itself. No one can ever use the excuse that they have been in a more trying circumstance than Christ.

Notice the intensity of the temptation in Gethsemane and at the cross. "As Christ felt His unity with the Father broken up, He feared that in His human nature He would be unable to endure the coming conflict with the powers of darkness. In the wilderness of temptation the destiny of the human race had been at stake. Christ was then conqueror. Now the tempter had come for the last fearful struggle. For this he had been preparing during the three years of Christ's ministry. Everything was at stake with him. If he failed here, his hope of mastery was lost; the kingdoms of the world would finally become Christ's; he himself would be overthrown and cast out. But if Christ could be overcome, the earth would become Satan's kingdom, and the human race would be forever in his power. With the issues of the conflict before Him, Christ's soul was filled with dread of separation from God" (*ibid.*, pp. 686, 687).

"Amid the awful darkness, apparently forsaken of God, Christ had drained the last dregs in the cup of human woe. In those dreadful hours He had relied upon the evidence of His Father's acceptance heretofore given Him. He was acquainted with the character of His Father; He understood His justice, His mercy, and His great love. By faith He rested in Him whom it had ever been His joy to obey. And as in submission He committed Himself to God, the sense of the loss of His Father's favor was withdrawn. By faith, Christ was victor" (*ibid.*, p. 756).

In spite of everything Satan attempted, Christ was victorious. "In every possible way Satan sought to prevent Jesus from developing a perfect childhood, a faultless manhood, a holy ministry, and an unblemished sacrifice. But he was defeated. He could not lead Jesus into sin. He could not discourage Him, or drive Him from the work He had come to this earth to do. From the desert to Calvary the storm of Satan's wrath beat upon Him, but the more mercilessly it fell, the more firmly did the Son of God cling to the hand of His Father, and press on in the blood-stained path" (*The Seventh-day Adventist Bible Commentary,* Ellen G. White Comments, vol. 5, p. 1130).

Yet Without Sin

Christ endured temptation in all points, "yet without sin" (Heb. 4:15). Scripture makes it clear that He had no sin. "Which of you convicts Me of sin?" (John 8:46). "The ruler of this world is coming, and he has nothing in Me" (John 14:30). "No unrighteousness is in Him" (John 7:18). "In Him there is no sin" (1 John 3:5). "The Holy One and the Just" (Acts 3:14). Christ "condemned sin in the flesh" (Rom. 8:3). Jesus "knew no sin" (2 Cor. 5:21) and was "holy, harmless, undefiled, separate from sinners" (Heb. 7:26). He "who committed no sin" (1 Peter 2:22) was "without blemish and without spot" (1 Peter 1:19). "On not one occasion was there a response to his manifold temptations. Not once did Christ step on Satan's ground, to give him any advantage. Satan found nothing in Him to encourage his advances" (*ibid.*, p. 1129).

The life of Christ is an example for us. He did not exercise any power not available to us, but relied totally upon His Father, thus gaining victory through submission and faith in God (*The Desire of Ages,* pp. 24, 130). Christ lived the life originally intended for us, a life in communion with God because He lived in harmony with God. Paul emphatically states that we may also overcome: "I can do all things through Christ who strengthens me" (Phil. 4:13; cf. Jude 24).

Died in Our Place

Christ, the divine Son of God, became one with us, not only to live for us and conquer where we had failed, but also to die in our place. Only He who was our Creator, who had life within Himself, could take our place. "The Lord has laid on Him the iniquity of us all" (Isa. 53:6). God "made Him who knew no sin to be sin for us, that we might become the righteousness of God in Him" (2 Cor. 5:21). Assuming upon Himself the sins that separated us from God, He Himself bore their consequences. He died our eternal death that we might receive His righteousness and life. Only in this way could God fulfill His original plan for our creation. And only by accepting His sacrifice do we have the opportunity of living in fellowship with God throughout eternity.

Resurrected for Us

Christ came not only to live for us and die in our place, but also to be resurrected on our behalf. While His death reconciles us, His life saves us (Rom. 5:10). Christ is the Son of God with power by virtue of His resurrection from the dead (Rom. 1:4). Baptism represents our participation in His death with its removal of our sins, in order that we might walk in a new life by virtue of His resurrection (Rom. 6:4; Col. 2:12, 13). The God who raised Jesus Christ from the dead is willing to give us the power of the resurrection in order that we might live for Him (Phil. 3:10; Heb. 13:20, 21; Rom. 8:11). We receive that resurrection power through faith (Phil. 3:9, 10).

Scripture clearly teaches that salvation is by faith alone. No amount of human effort can save us. In fact, to seek salvation by works is itself sinful, for it is an attempt to live independently, autonomously from God. However, "Do we then make void [God's] law through faith? Certainly not! On the contrary, we establish the law" (Rom. 3:31). By faith we accept the reconciliation with God made possible by Christ's death, and also by faith we accept the power of His resurrection. God gives forgiveness not that we might continue in sin, but in order that we might be reconciled to God. If we willfully continue to sin, we continually break our connection with Him, thereby nullifying the purpose of Christ's death. The foundation of our salvation is always by grace through faith, but the result of salvation is life in Jesus Christ by faith in the power of His resurrection. Therefore, faith establishes the possibility of living in harmony with God.

The First Coming Prepares for the Second

Paul makes a clear connection between the death of Christ and the life we live as we await the Second Coming: "For the grace of God that brings salvation has appeared to all men, teaching us that, denying ungodliness and worldly lusts, we should live soberly, righteously, and godly in the present age, looking for the blessed hope and glorious appearing of our great God and Savior Jesus Christ, who gave Himself for us, that He might redeem us from every lawless deed and purify for Himself His own special people, zealous for good works" (Titus 2:11-14).

The Bible makes many other connections between the first coming of Christ and the certainty of His return. The book of Acts assures us that Jesus will return in the same manner as He went into heaven (Acts 1:9-11). Christ Himself linked His first advent with His return for us: "Let not your heart be troubled;

you believe in God, believe also in Me. In My Father's house are many mansions; if it were not so, I would have told you. I go to prepare a place for you. And if I go and prepare a place for you, I will come again and receive you to Myself; that where I am, there you may be also" (John 14:1-3).

Christ is the firstfruits of those who will be resurrected at the Second Coming (1 Cor. 15:23). He is the one who was dead, but now is alive forevermore and has the keys of death and the grave (Rev. 1:18). "So Christ was offered once to bear the sins of many. To those who eagerly wait for Him He will appear a second time, apart from sin, for salvation" (Heb. 9:28). Our hope of the resurrection at the Second Coming also depends upon our faith in the resurrection of Christ (1 Cor. 15:12-19). Himself inherently immortal, Christ desires to give everlasting life to us. Only if we have a relationship with the Son will we have everlasting life (1 John 5:11, 12). It is available to those who have faith. "For if we believe that Jesus died and rose again, even so God will bring with him those who sleep in Jesus. For this we say to you by the word of the Lord, that we who are alive and remain until the coming of the Lord will by no means precede those who are asleep. For the Lord Himself will descend from heaven with a shout, with the voice of an archangel, and with the trumpet of God. And the dead in Christ will rise first. Then we who are alive and remain shall be caught up together with them in the clouds to meet the Lord in the air. And thus we shall always be with the Lord" (1 Thess. 4:14-17; cf. 2 Cor. 4:14).

Having retained His humanity even after the Resurrection, Christ will be one with us throughout eternity. He is more closely united with us now than if He had never walked with us in the flesh (*The Desire of Ages,* p. 25). After He rose from the dead, Christ did not return in some spirit form but in the flesh. He ate food (Luke 24:38-43) and showed the disciples His hands and His side, inviting them to physically touch Him (John 20:20, 27). The bodily resurrection of our Lord illustrates our own resurrection. We will not rise from the grave as spirits but will be complete human beings with bodies. The bodily resurrection of Christ protects our concept of the unity of human nature. It con-

THE FIRST COMING PREPARES FOR . . .

firms that it always takes the combination of the spirit and the body to form a living soul.

Sometimes we may struggle with many questions. What if Jesus were not divine? What if He did not become a human? What if He had not been faithful to the point of death? What if He had not been victorious? What if Christ did not come the first time? But as a matter of fact, Christ *did* come and *was* faithful—therefore we can have confidence in the Second Coming! His advent reestablished the relationship between God and humanity, and His second coming culminates it.

Christ set a pattern for those preparing for the Second Coming. Choosing to live His life within the context of the Word of God by the power of God, He led the way by rejecting the life that leads to independence from God. Rather, He overcame as we must. "It is written" was His motto. He let neither the evidences of His senses nor the misleading rationalizations of philosophy sway Him, thereby setting an example for those who live in the last days (*The Great Controversy,* p. 625). The major issue in the last days will be our relationship to the Word of God. Will we take it as the foundation under all other authorities, or will we substitute for it ecclesiastical bodies, political institutions, science, or the spirit world? God will have a people on earth who will follow Christ and accept the Bible and the Bible only! (*ibid.,* p. 595). Are we ready to stand with Christ and the remnant by faith in God's Word, or do we wish to assert our own authority? Do we insist on creating our own designer gods, or do we accept the God who has revealed Himself in Jesus Christ and His Word, the Bible?

Imagine yourself in the position of Christ, seeking to woo back your own. You long to restore to fellowship all those separated from you. Yet when you burst upon the world as light shining into darkness, the darkness did not understand you. Although they were your people, they ignored you, preferring darkness and hiding themselves from the light. Although you were the Creator, they did not know you, let alone worship you. Even though you were the truth, they questioned you. They scorned your birth, despised you, mocked you, beat you, placed a crown of thorns upon your head, and finally crucified you. Though you

THE CERTAINTY OF THE SECOND COMING

died as substitute for their sins, they responded with indifference and ingratitude. And yet you did not react with anger or revenge—you wept over them and cried out in despair, "What more could I have done for My vineyard? O, Jerusalem, Jerusalem, how I would have gathered your children together, but you were unwilling" (Matt. 23:37).

Such love and devotion is beyond our comprehension. Philosophy cannot explain it, archaeology cannot discover it, science cannot dissect it. Yet God freely gives it to us. We can cling to our designer gods and thereby shut that love out from our lives and thereby cut ourselves off from the Life-giver. Or we can fulfill God's purpose in sending His Son to live and die for us by opening our lives to His self-revelation and love. By so doing, we will affirm our participation in the Second Coming and our fellowship with God and fellow human beings throughout eternity.

Chapter 6

Salvation and the Certainty of the Second Coming

SUPPOSE THAT the universe assigned you the job of designing the plan of salvation. What elements would you weave into the proposal? Would you prescribe a journey to some faraway holy place, or a climb to the top of a hallowed mountain? Should the proposal include the eating of some sacred food, or receiving the blessing of a pious person? Would you consider some feat of valor, the gift or even sacrifice of something treasured, the self-denial of some important aspect of life, or the abandonment of something accumulated during a lifetime? Maybe a special form of meditation, a chant, the offering of some incense, or a specified set of mental gymnastics would do. Perhaps acceptance and mastery of a set of beliefs, or the memorization of a sacred text would suffice. You could consider the observance of a prescribed set of laws or devise a system to use sleight of hand or words to fool the gods into granting salvation.

Or you could develop a system that is more proactive, basing salvation not on some qualification, but participation in the process of bringing about God's kingdom on earth. People could accomplish it through humanitarian efforts to relieve suffering, by education to give them the tools to achieve their own better life, or by involvement in social or political revolution, perhaps a "just war" intended to eliminate unfair systems. Salvation would depend upon a future created by humanity itself.

And what kind of gods would fit into your master proposal? Would they be vindictive or loving, distant or near, powerful or weak, manipulatable or immovable, legalistic or pragmatic, omniscient or limited in knowledge? Surely whatever the plan, it would include a "designer god"—one who knew how to behave in harmony with the best ethics achieved by your society. A sophisticated god for a sophisticated age, it would be a god of love but would not come to die in our place, for it is unthinkably unjust for one person to die for another. It might live and finally die as a manifestation of ultimate love, but not as a propitiation for our sins, for that would be "paganism," a step backward for such an elite society. Such a god must have an approach appropriate with our advanced culture.

Perhaps you might consider an ultimate god of love, one who will grant salvation to all regardless of their commitment. A god who either has no laws or looks the other way when someone breaks them. It would be a doting deity who excuses any behavior of its children and exhibits infinite love and infinite tolerance.

But it is time for us to stop our daydreaming. No one has given us the job of developing such a proposal. God is who He is, and He alone is in charge of the plan of salvation. Whether we like it or not, it is not our business to tell Him how to run His universe. In fact, that is the very act that got Satan into trouble in the first place. Our role is not to prescribe how He can appropriately save us, but to accept graciously His self-revelation and His plan for our salvation.

As sinful humans, it is our nature to attempt to build our own god(s). Isaiah describes a woodsman who chops down a tree. After using a portion of the tree to construct part of his home, he builds a fire and cooks a meal with another segment. Then, with what is left, he whittles a god and bows down to worship it. If we can create our own god, then we can control that deity, and thereby assure our own salvation.

However, we are not in control of our own destiny, for we have all sinned and fall short of who God is (Rom. 3:23). "There is none righteous, no, not one; there is none who understands; there is none who seeks after God. They have all turned aside; they have together become unprofitable; there is none who does good, no, not one" (verses 10-12). As sinners, our natures clash with that of God (Rom. 8:7) to the point that we are even His enemies (Rom. 5:10). We are out of work when it comes to the task of creating a "designer god" complete with blueprints on how to run the plan of salvation. In fact, we are not even in a negotiating position with Him to discuss its terms. Like a branch cut off from the vine, or the lamb separated from the sheepfold, we find ourselves helplessly in sin.

The fact that we are sinners separates us from the Life-giver. As Scripture puts it, the wages of sin is death (Rom. 6:23; cf. Gen. 2:17). However, God created us for life, for fellowship with Him! Sin and death thwarted His purposes in our creation. God desires to give us life rather than death, because only in life can we fellowship with Him. Therefore, God Himself chose the manner by which He would save His people from their sins (Matt. 1:21; Acts 2:23; 1 Peter 1:20). "For God so loved the world that He gave His only begotten Son, that whoever believes in Him should not perish but have everlasting life. For God did not send His Son into the world to condemn the world, but that the world through Him might be saved" (John 3:16, 17). While "the wages of sin is death, . . . the gift of God is eternal life in Christ Jesus our Lord" (Rom. 6:23).

Planning Salvation

God Himself established the plan for our salvation. It really does not matter whether or not it seems reasonable to us or our culture. He says that "without shedding of blood there is no remission" of sins (Heb. 9:22). Because God desired to give us life, He "laid on Him the iniquity of us all" (Isa. 53:6). Therefore, Christ became a sacrifice to bear our sins (Heb. 9:22, 23) as God redeemed us "with the precious blood of Christ, as of a lamb without blemish and without spot" (1 Peter 1:19). Christ bore our sins in His own body on the symbolic tree (the cross) in order that He might bring us to God (1 Peter 2:24; 3:18). The cross demonstrates God's love to us as He "sent His Son to be the propitiation for our sins" (1 John 4:10; cf. 1 John 2:2; Rom. 3:25).

"Now all things are of God, who has reconciled us to Himself through Jesus Christ, . . . that is, that God was in Christ reconciling the world to Himself, not imputing their trespasses to them. . . . For He made Him who knew no sin to be sin for us, that we might become the righteous of God in Him" (2 Cor. 5:18-21). This gift of love came not only from God the Father, but also from Jesus Himself. "Christ also has loved us and given Himself for us, an offering and a sacrifice to God for a sweet-smelling aroma" (Eph. 5:2; cf. Col. 1:20-22).

"Christ was treated as we deserve, that we might be treated as He deserves. He was condemned for our sins, in which He had no share, that we might be justified by His righteousness, in which we had no share. He suffered the death which was ours, that we might receive the life which was His. 'With His stripes we are healed'" (*The Desire of Ages,* p. 25).

The Bible clearly states that only the substitutionary death of Christ makes our salvation possible. Some reject this biblical teaching because it flies in the face of the "moral sensibility" of our age. If we cannot trust the Bible when it describes God's plan for our salvation, then we must also question its credibility on the Second Coming. Rejection of the propitiatory death of Christ leaves us without the biblical promise of His return.

The cross reveals the horror of sin and demonstrates the depth to which Satan and sinners will go. When given the opportunity, they will slay the very Son of God! The cross also portrays God's judgment on sin. So terrible that it requires the death of the sinner, sin must be eradicated from the universe. God the Father and the Lamb turn their wrath against sin and those who wallow in it (Rom. 5:9; Rev. 6:17).

The cross also displays the depth of God's love. Refusing to sidestep the sin issue, He will confront it head-on. But at the same time He will accept the penalty Himself in order to give us life. "God demonstrates His own love toward us, in that while we were still sinners, Christ died for us" (Rom. 5:8). But in so doing God the Father and God the Son took the risk of eternal separation from each other. The Son assumed our nature in order to live as we must even though it meant the possibility of sinning and being severed from the Father. At the cross Christ experienced the isolation from God that the sinner will experience in the final destruction at the end of the millennium (Matt. 27:46). The Majesty of heaven became one with us in order to die in our place so that He might restore us to eternal life and fellowship with God.

A Free Gift

Salvation is God's gift rather than our achievement. It has its origin in God's design rather than in our wisdom or efforts (1 Cor. 1:21; 2 Tim. 1:9). No human activity will ever justify anyone in God's sight (Rom. 3:20) for Christ "has saved us and called us with a holy calling, not according to our works, but according to His own purpose and grace which was given to us in Christ Jesus before time began" (2 Tim. 1:9; cf. Rom. 5:15-21). If salvation results from anything we do, "then it is no longer of works; otherwise grace is no longer grace. But if it is of works, it is no longer grace; otherwise work is no longer work" (Rom. 11:6). Paul reassures us that "by grace you have been saved" (Eph. 2:8; cf. Rom. 3:24).

How do we have access to God's saving grace? By faith (Rom. 5:2; Gal. 3:22; Gen. 15:6). If we did not receive salvation by faith, then it would not be of grace (Rom. 4:16) but something else, such as works, wisdom, or meditation. Although salvation is a free gift from God, saving faith does have content and a definite focus. We have to trust that God has indeed provided redemption by setting forth Christ Jesus as a propitiation through His death on the cross (Rom. 3:24, 25). Further, if we confess our allegiance to Jesus, and believe that God has raised Him from the dead, God will save us (Rom. 10:8, 9; John 11:25-27). When we by faith accept Jesus Christ as our Saviour, then God gives us the power to become sons of God (John 1:12). The truly just shall live by faith, or total trust, in God (Rom. 1:17; Heb. 10:38, 39).

If salvation is a freely offered gift from God that we must accept by faith (Eph. 2:8), it is important for us to know what faith itself is. We have already seen that it is not our job to develop a designer concept of salvation. Salvation is God's gift rather than our creation. If that is the case, then we must allow God the privilege of defining the nature of faith. In chapter 8 we will see that faith does not have a human origin, but comes through the power of God's Word under the Holy Spirit.

Salvation ceases to be a gift if it is received by a faith that itself rests upon a rational, scientific, or historical argument just as it would cease to be a gift if it had its basis in human works. Humanity's natural tendency is to desire to accept God and His salvation from a position of independence. But any attempt to do that only represents a continued rebellion against God. We must rely upon the Word of God rather than upon human philosophy. "Our salvation depends on a knowledge of the truth contained in the Scriptures" (*Christ's Object Lessons,* p. 111).

Salvation and the Certainty of the Second Coming

The Bible intimately connects the themes of the authority of the Bible, salvation by grace through faith, resurrection to newness of life, living an obedient life, and the Second Coming. Note, for example, the following passage from Peter: "Blessed be the God and Father of our Lord Jesus Christ, who according to His abundant mercy has *begotten us* again to a *living hope* through the *resurrection of Jesus Christ* from the dead, to an *inheritance* incorruptible and undefiled and that does not fade away, reserved in *heaven* for you, who are *kept by the power of God* through *faith for salvation* ready to be *revealed in the last time.* In this you greatly rejoice, though now for a little while, if need be, you have been grieved by various trials, that the *genuineness of your faith,* being much more precious than gold that perishes, though it is tested by fire, may be found to praise, honor, and glory at the *revelation of Jesus Christ,* whom having not seen you love. Though now you do not see Him, yet *believing,* you rejoice with joy inexpressible and full of glory, receiving *the end of your faith—the salvation of your souls.* Of this *salvation* the *prophets* have inquired and searched carefully, who *prophesied of the grace* that would come to you, searching what, or what manner of time, *the Spirit of Christ who was in them was indicating when He testified beforehand the sufferings of Christ and the glories that would follow.* To them it was *revealed* that, not to themselves, but to us *they were ministering the things which now have been reported to you through those who have preached the gospel to you by the Holy Spirit sent from heaven—things which angels*

SALVATION

desire to look into. Therefore *gird up the loins of your mind, be sober,* and rest your *hope fully* upon the *grace* that is to be brought to you at the *revelation of Jesus Christ*; as *obedient* children, *not conforming yourselves to the former lusts*, as in your ignorance; but as He who called you is *holy*, you also be *holy* in all your conduct, because it is written, '*Be holy, for I am holy.*' And if you call on the Father, who without partiality judges according to each one's work, *conduct* yourselves throughout the time of your stay here in fear; knowing that you were not *redeemed* with corruptible things, like silver or gold, from your *aimless conduct* received by tradition from your fathers, but with the *precious blood of Christ,* as of a lamb without blemish and without spot. He indeed was *foreordained* before the foundation of the world, but was manifest in these last times for you who through Him *believe* in God, who *raised* Him from the dead and gave Him glory, so that *your faith* and *hope* are in God. Since you have *purified* your souls in *obeying the truth* through the Spirit in sincere love of the brethren, *love* one another fervently with a pure heart, having been *born again,* not of corruptible seed but incorruptible, through the *word of God* which lives and abides forever, because 'All flesh is as grass, and all the glory of man as the flower of the grass. The grass withers, and its flower falls away, but the *word of the Lord* endures forever.' Now this is the word which by the *gospel* was preached to you" (1 Peter 1:3-25; cf. 2 Tim. 1:9, 10; Titus 3:4-7; Heb. 6:12; 11:5).

Paul puts it this way: "Christ was offered once to bear the sins of many. To those who eagerly wait for Him He will appear a second time, apart from sin, for salvation" (Heb. 9:28). Christ Himself said: "No one can come to Me unless the Father who sent Me draws him; and I will raise him up at the last day" (John 6:44).

The biblical doctrine of salvation emphasizes the fact that Christianity is a relationship with God. He wants to restore the face-to-face intimacy that we originally had in the garden of Eden. God longs to walk with us and talk with us as a friend. "Behold, I stand at the door and knock. If anyone hears My voice and opens the door, I will come in to him and dine with him, and he with Me" (Rev. 3:20). Our Lord planned even before our creation to offer restoration should sin ever separate us from Him. He would take the results of sin (death resulting from being cut off from the Life-giver) upon Himself in order that in Jesus Christ we might be reunited with Him. The Lord thereby both demonstrated the perpetuity of the law as a guide to healthy relationships and made possible a way by which He might reestablish our relationship with Him. The culmination of our salvation takes place at the Second Coming when we will be reunited with God face-to-face.

Forgiveness Restores

God, offering us restoration, longs for us to accept His invitation. "If we confess our sins, He is faithful and just to forgive us our sins and to cleanse us from all unrighteousness" (1 John 1:9). Should we fall into sin again, He still stands there, eager to offer pardon. "I write to you, so that you may not sin. And if anyone sins, we have an Advocate with the Father, Jesus Christ the righteous" (1 John 2:1). But His plan of restoration is not effective unless we accept it.

Perhaps you recall a time when a close friend did you wrong. It disrupted your relationship. Out of a desire to restore the relationship, you offered forgiveness. But your friend refused it. He or she could have rejected your offer of forgiveness for many reasons. Perhaps the individual was too proud, feeling that he or she was above the need for forgiveness or that the act was too trivial to require it or that no wrong had been done in the first place. Or your friend might have rejected the forgiveness out of fear that the offer was not genuine. At the other extreme, the person could have felt too unworthy to accept the forgiveness, as if the magnitude of the trespass was too great to be forgiven. Whatever the case, it thwarted your desire to restore the relationship, not because you didn't offer forgiveness, but because the other person did not accept it.

When my wife, Ann, and I were first married, my mother gave us a silver-gray toy poodle named Jolly. She was an adorable outgoing dog, and well housebroken. One day when we returned home, though, we missed her usual vivacious and friendly greeting as we entered the front door. We called and searched for her, but could not find her anywhere. After carefully searching the house, we found *it,* and then knew why she had disappeared. After cleaning up the doggie mess, we called again, and finally found her crouched under the piano bench. Regardless of our coaxing and our offer of forgiveness, she continued to cower under the piano bench, refusing to let us pick her up. We had extended forgiveness because we wanted to restore the relationship. But it remained severed for a time because she refused to accept our offer.

We as human beings may also reject God's forgiveness for any number of reasons. No matter what the reason, our refusal to accept it blocks God's desire to restore us to Himself. How often as Christians do we remain crouched under the piano bench because we do not accept God's offer of forgiveness!

Our God forgives! "Who is a God like You, pardoning iniquity and passing over the transgression of the remnant of His heritage? He does not retain His anger forever, because He delights in mercy. He will again have compassion on us, and will subdue our iniquities. You will cast all our sins into the depths of the sea" (Micah 7:18, 19). God wants to separate our sins from us as far as the east is from the west!

Have you ever attempted to maintain a relationship with someone when you did not know where you stood with the person? You were always on edge, not knowing whether the other individual accepted you or not. It was difficult—if not impossible—to get close to the person. God does not want us to live in fear of our relationship with Him. Longing for us to know where we stand with Him, He desires that we have peace and confidence in our relationship with Him. "Therefore, having been justified by faith, we have peace with God through our Lord Jesus Christ" (Rom. 5:1). "He who believes in the Son of God has the witness in himself; he who does not believe God has made Him a liar, because he has not believed the testimony that God has given of His Son. And this is the testimony: that God has given us eternal life, and this life is in His Son. He who has the Son has life; he who does not have the Son of God does not have life. These things I have written to you who believe in the name of the Son of God, that you may know that you have eternal life, and that you may continue to believe in the name of the Son of God" (1 John 5:10-14).

God asks us to come boldly by faith before His throne (Heb. 4:16). Wanting our fellowship now, He longs that we will have the assurance of the Second Coming because He desires to meet us face-to-face at the Second Coming so that we can walk with Him throughout eternity!

Chapter 7

The Sanctuary and the Second Coming

SEVENTH-DAY ADVENTISTS believe that an investigative judgment will take place in heaven just prior to the Second Coming.* This judgment started in 1844 in fulfillment of the prophecy of Daniel 8:14 about the cleansing of the sanctuary. The model of the ancient earthly Israelite sanctuary illustrates what takes place in the heavenly one. As in Old Testament times people by faith placed their sins upon the sin offering and through its blood their sins were symbolically transferred to the earthly sanctuary, so in the new covenant the sins of the repentant are placed by faith upon Christ and transferred to the heavenly sanctuary. And as the removal of the sins polluting it cleansed the earthly sanctuary, so God will accomplish the actual cleansing of the heavenly by the removal, or blotting out, of the sins recorded there. But before that can take place, someone must examine heaven's records to determine who, through repentance of sin and faith in Christ, are entitled to the benefits of Christ's atonement. The cleansing of the sanctuary therefore involves an investigative function—a work of judgment. It must occur prior to the coming of Christ to redeem His people, for when He arrives, He will reward every person according to what he or she has done in life (Rev. 22:12; *The Great Controversy*, pp. 421, 422).

Paul declared that "we must all appear before the judgment seat of Christ, that each one may receive the things done in the body, according to what he has done, whether good or bad" (2 Cor. 5:10). For God "has appointed a day on which He will judge the world in righteousness by the Man whom He has ordained" (Acts 17:31). Daniel graphically describes the scene: "I watched till thrones were put in place, and the Ancient of Days was seated; his garment was white as snow, and the hair of His head was like pure wool. His throne was a fiery flame, its wheels a burning fire; A fiery stream issued and came forth from before Him. A thousand thousands ministered to Him; ten thousand times ten thousand stood before Him. The court was seated, and the books were opened" (Dan. 7:9, 10). The judgment will consider every deed (Eccl. 12:13, 14; Rev. 20:12).

The standard of judgment is God's law (James 2:10-12). "The record of every life is written in the books of heaven. Every sin that has been committed is there registered. Every regret for sin, every tear of repentance, every confession of guilt, and the forsaking of every darling sin, is also recorded. When the judgment shall sit and the books are opened, every case will have to stand the test of the law of God. God has a law by which He governs intelligences both in heaven and in earth. Jehovah is the supreme Governor of nations, and no greater or more fatal deception could take hold on human minds than that which leads men to declare that the law of God has been abolished. Were this so there could be no judgment; for there would be no rule by which character could be tested, and actions weighed. But we read that the judgment is to sit, and that the books are to be opened, and that every man is to be rewarded according as his works have been. If God has no moral standard by which to measure character, there can be no judgment, no reward" (*Signs of the Times,* May 16, 1895).

Three Phases of Judgment

The divine judgment has three phases. The first is the investigative judgment. The messages of the three angels in Revelation 14 announce that the hour of God's judgment has arrived. Therefore, it has to take place just before the second coming of Christ. The second phase involves the judgment of the wicked during the millennium, and the third or executive phase of the judgment will happen at the end of the millennium when God destroys sin and sinners. The last two phases of judgment will be our study in chapter 12.

The whole idea of the investigative judgment may confuse

those who desire to test it on the basis of human reasonableness. They raise a number of questions: Is it really necessary for God to conduct an investigative judgment since He already knows everything? If He forgives sins at the time of our repentance, why would God wait until the judgment to blot them out? Since God saves us by grace, why then does He judge us by His law? What relevance to my life is a judgment taking place in heaven?

It is tempting to argue that since we can find no good reason that God should have such a judgment, and since the idea of one seems to contradict the gospel, we can therefore safely conclude that no investigative judgment currently takes place in heaven. In effect, we dictate the terms under which God can operate. We argue, "God, whatever You do must make sense to me. If it doesn't, I will assume that You're not doing any such thing." By so arguing, we put ourselves in judgment upon God and thus echo humanity's sin in Eden. We doubt the Word of God and elevate our own philosophy in its place, bowing in worship before a designer god of our own making.

The Judgment Turned Upside Down

Some theologies actually turn the judgment upside down. They regard it as a time when the universe judges God Himself, seeing Him on trial during the time of the investigative judgment, at the judgment that takes place during the millennium, and at the destruction of the wicked at the end of the millennium. Is God truly the epitome of love, justice, truth, and freedom? Can the universe trust Him to live by these eternal principles? Can He be relied upon to govern by them throughout eternity? (See chapter 13.)

The model for such a theology comes from Western political and educational philosophy in which freedom is king. It considers God as successful in the universe in the same sense that a president succeeds in a democratic state or that an idea gains acceptance in a university. He makes His way in the universe by persuasion of "truth."

The task of the great tribunal before which God will stand is to determine the principles of truth, so that it can then judge

THE CERTAINTY OF THE SECOND COMING

Him. The participants in the trial will extrapolate from their study of nature, history, and interpersonal relationships the basic principles by which the universe operates. The principles will then serve as the basis for measuring the "truth about God."

Such theologies assume that God is the epitome or highest expression of truth, love, justice, and freedom. As the highest manifestation of these principles, He can be tested or measured by them.

What have we done to God when we attempt to bring Him into judgment? If we find "principles of truth" by which to measure God, is God the one measured or the one who measures? Actually, we construct out of our philosophy an idol, a designer god, that we then compare against God! In this scenario the God of the universe becomes subordinate to the universe itself and, it would seem, to the ones who judge Him. Such concepts run the risk of testing the Word of God as did Eve. It is the same mistake the antediluvians made prior to the Flood, and Israel at Kadesh-barnea. A determination to question God lay behind the attempt to subvert Christ's loyalty in the wilderness. "Has God not said?" asked the serpent. The clearly implied answer is no—at least it is not reasonable if He did. "I will tell Him how He should operate in His universe."

Such theologies must come under the test of Scripture rather than the other way around. We must not judge Scripture on the basis of a concept of freedom arising from the enlightenment. Rather, we must bring contemporary concepts of freedom, truth, love, and justice to the standard of Scripture.

Who Is Our Judge?

Who is this God whom we intend to judge? He is the Creator of the universe, the great I AM. He has life within Himself, and is therefore the Giver of life. Instead of being the epitome of freedom, love, truth, and justice, He is their foundation. He is the measure, rather than Someone subject to their measure. Without Him we would not know freedom, love, truth, and justice.

Isaiah makes it clear that God is unsearchable (Isa. 40:28). We cannot compare Him to anything or anyone, nor is anyone His equal (verses 18, 25). Certain theologies assume that God can be measured by and compared to the "principles" that finite beings extrapolate from the universe, but Isaiah declares that God makes the judges of the earth useless (verse 23). None of us are in a position to direct the Spirit of the Lord, to counsel Him, to teach Him justice or knowledge (verses 13, 14). No one has the authority to declare Him righteous or not (Isa. 41:26-29). As Paul emphasized, His judgments are unsearchable (Rom. 11:33).

God's creatures have not been given the task of bringing judgment upon Him (Job 40:2, 8; Rom. 9:20, 21; Isa. 40:23). The task of judgment is God's prerogative. It is He who operates through His Son to judge the world. "For He is coming, for He is coming to judge the earth. He shall judge the world with righteousness, and the people with His truth" (Ps. 96:13). "But with righteousness He shall judge the poor, and decide with equity for the meek of the earth; He shall strike the earth with the rod of His mouth, and with the breath of His lips He shall slay the wicked" (Isa. 11:4). "A fiery stream issued and came forth from before Him. A thousand thousands ministered to Him; ten thousand times ten thousand stood before Him. The court was seated, and the books were opened" (Dan. 7:10; cf. Ps. 94:2; 96:13; John 5:22, 27, 30; Acts 10:42; 17:31; Rom. 2:16; Rev. 19:11). The Father has committed all judgment to the Son (John 5:22). The Son's judgment is just because it has come from the Father (verses 19, 20, 30).

"It is He, the source of all being, and the foundation of all law, that is to preside in the judgment" (*The Great Controversy*, p. 479). Ellen White warns against those who "presume to pass sentence upon God's moral government" (*Patriarchs and Prophets*, p. 124). "He does not lay open His plans to prying, inquisitive minds. We must not attempt to lift with presumptuous hand the curtain behind which He veils His majesty. . . . No mortal mind can penetrate the secrecy in which the Mighty One dwells and works. We can comprehend no more of His dealings with us and the motives that actuate Him than He sees fit to reveal. He orders everything in righteousness, and we are not to be dissatisfied and distrustful, but to bow in reverent submission" (*Testimonies*, vol. 5, pp. 301, 302).

The desire to bring God into judgment is at the root of the sin problem. It arises from the temptation to live our lives independently of God, the attempt to go it alone, to know our own truth, to determine our own morality, and to live by our own wisdom, a wisdom so haughty that it claims the right to judge God!

God Reveals His Righteousness

It is not our place to put God in the crucible of our judgment. God's justice does not depend upon our verdict, because "the judgments of the Lord are true and righteous altogether" (Ps. 19:9). God is a righteous Judge (Rom. 2:5; 2 Tim. 4:8). How do we know, if we ourselves are not the litmus test for His righteousness? God will *reveal* His righteousness. "The Lord has made known His salvation; His righteousness He has revealed in the sight of the nations. . . . For He is coming to judge the earth. With righteousness He shall judge the world, and the peoples with equity" (Ps. 98:2-9). Notice that it is not we who justify God (Rom. 14:12), but God who justifies us. In spite of our sinfulness, God has revealed His righteousness, a revelation witnessed in the Law (the books of Moses) and the Prophets. The manifestation of God's righteousness in the gift of Jesus Christ as our propitiation is the basis upon which through faith we also might be justified (Rom. 3:21-27). The gospel reveals His righteousness (Rom. 1:16, 17) not our wisdom (1 Cor. 1:21). The conviction that He is indeed righteousness is not our doing, but the role of the Holy Spirit (John 16:8).

We do not receive a revelation from God on the basis of human wisdom, but upon the power of God (1 Cor. 1). Thus at the end of the millennium every knee will bow at the revelation of God's righteousness. Every tongue shall "confess that Jesus Christ is Lord, to the glory of God the Father" (Phil 2:11; cf. verses 9, 10; Isa. 45:16-25; Rom. 14:9-12).

Ellen White also emphasizes the revelatory nature of our acceptance of the righteousness of God. Notice the italicized sections of the following quotation: "But many mysteries yet remain *unre-*

vealed. How much that is acknowledged to be truth is mysterious and *unexplainable to the human mind!* How dark seem the dispensations of Providence! What necessity there is for *implicit faith* and trust in God's moral government! We are ready to say with Paul, 'How *unsearchable* are his judgments, and his ways past finding out!'

"We are not now sufficiently advanced in spiritual attainments to comprehend the mysteries of God. But when we shall compose the family of heaven, these mysteries will be *unfolded* before us. Of the members of that family John writes: 'They shall hunger no more, neither thirst any more; neither shall the sun light on them, nor any heat. For the Lamb which is in the midst of the throne shall *feed* them, and shall *lead* them unto living fountains of waters: and God shall wipe away all tears from their eyes.' 'And they shall see his face; and his name shall be in their foreheads.'

"Then much *will be revealed in explanation* of matters upon which God now keeps silence because we have not gathered up and appreciated that which has been made known of the eternal mysteries. The ways of Providence *will be made clear;* the mysteries of grace through Christ will be *unfolded*. That which the mind cannot now grasp, which is hard to be understood, *will be explained*. We shall see order in that which has seemed unexplainable; wisdom in everything withheld; goodness and gracious mercy in everything *imparted*. Truth will be *unfolded* to the mind, free from obscurity, in a single line, and its brightness will be endurable. The heart *will be made* to sing for joy.

"Controversies will be forever ended, and all difficulties will be solved" (*The Seventh-day Adventist Bible Commentary,* Ellen G. White Comments, vol. 6, p. 1091; italics supplied).

The major issue in the great controversy between Christ and Satan is our relationship to the Word of God. Will we call the Word of God into question as did Eve, or will we live by it as did Christ? We find ourselves tempted to question God and His Word even in the way we set up our theology. The idea that we bring God into judgment elevates us to a position equal to or above God. We determine the measure by which God is to be judged. The following is a comparison of the two positions:

THE CERTAINTY OF THE SECOND COMING

The universe is judge	***God is judge***
The "judgment" is the judgment of the universe on God.	The "judgment" is the judgment of God on sin and sinners.
God's actions pass in review before the great tribunal of the universe.	Our lives pass in review before the Judge of all the earth.
We hold Him up to the eternal standard of truth, love, justice, and freedom.	We accept Him as the source and standard of truth, love, justice, and freedom.
We question His judgments.	We accept His judgments.
We are independent from Christ.	We are slaves of Satan, but become free in Jesus.
Knowledge is independent of God.	God provides the foundation of knowledge.
We see God with reference to the law of the universe.	We see ourselves with reference to the law of God, and accept God's judgment on our sin.
Sin is the transgression of the laws inherent in the universe.	Sin is the transgression of the character of God.
We live by what remains after we have made a human judgment on the Word of God.	We live by every word that proceeds out of the mouth of God.
We determine whether "god" is truth, righteousness, and love.	God reveals His glory, truth, righteousness, and love.

What manner of "god" ought he to be in our presence?	What manner of persons ought we to be in God's presence?
We create a designer god out of our own image.	We accept the God who reveals Himself.

God does not win the universe by the force of human logic, reason, or sense experience. "If they do not hear Moses and the prophets, neither will they be persuaded though one rise from the dead" (Luke 16:31). God restores the universe to Himself by the revelation of His love. "The earth was dark through misapprehension of God. That the gloomy shadows might be lightened, that the world might be brought back to God, Satan's deceptive power was to be broken. This could not be done by force. The exercise of force is contrary to the principles of God's government; He desires only the service of love; and love cannot be commanded; it cannot be won by force or authority. Only by love is love awakened. To know God is to love Him; His character must be manifested in contrast to the character of Satan. This work only one Being in all the universe could do. Only He who knew the height and depth of the love of God could make it known. Upon the world's dark night the Sun of Righteousness must rise, 'with healing in His wings.' Mal. 4:2" (*The Desire of Ages*, p. 22).

The Good News of Judgment

If the investigative judgment is God's judgment on sin and sinners, then some might express concerns about whether God operates out of a motive of love in the judgment. Does He seek to terrorize us with the judgment somewhat as the doctrine of an ever-burning hell has frightened the generations of Christians who have held that unbiblical concept? Has God told us about the judgment to goad us into living righteously? Does He want us to live in fear regarding our relationship with Him and His desires for us? The biblical message is that the judgment is part of the everlasting gospel—it is good news!

Why is it great news? Because our Friend, the one who came to save us, who longs to take us home to live with Him eternally, stands by our side in court as our high priest, intercessor, substitute, judge, witness, and advocate. No wonder we are to come boldly before the throne of grace! (Heb. 4:16; 7:27; 1 John 2:1; John 5:22, 27, 30).

David looked forward to God's judgment: "He shall judge the peoples righteously. Let the heavens rejoice, and let the earth be glad; let the sea roar, and all its fullness; let the field be joyful, and all that is in it. Then all the trees of the woods will rejoice before the Lord. For He is coming, for He is coming to judge the earth. He shall judge the world with righteousness, and the peoples with His truth" (Ps. 96:10-13; cf. 26:1; 43:1). Well might David rejoice, for judgment will be "made in favor of the saints of the Most High" and the time will come for the saints to possess the kingdom (Dan. 7:22; cf. Zech. 3:2).

The psalmist encourages us to sing praises to God in view of the judgment: "Oh, sing to the Lord a new song! For He has done marvelous things; His right hand and His holy arm have gained Him the victory. The Lord has made known His salvation; His righteousness He has revealed in the sight of the nations. He has remembered His mercy and His faithfulness to the house of Israel; all the ends of the earth have seen the salvation of our God. Shout joyfully to the Lord, all the earth; break forth in song, rejoice, and sing praises. Sing to the Lord with the harp, with the harp and the sound of a psalm, with trumpets and the sound of a horn; shout joyfully before the Lord, the King. Let the sea roar, and all its fullness, the world and those who dwell in it; let the rivers clap their hands; let the hills be joyful together before the Lord, for He is coming to judge the earth. With righteousness He shall judge the world, and the peoples with equity" (Ps. 98:1-9; cf. Isa. 40:4-11).

Ezekiel brings God's promise of cleansing: "Then I will sprinkle clean water on you, and you shall be clean; I will cleanse you from all your filthiness and from all your idols. I will give you a new heart and put a new spirit within you; I will take the heart of stone out of your flesh and give you a heart of flesh. I will put

THE SANCTUARY

My Spirit within you and cause you to walk in My statutes, and you will keep My judgments and do them. Then you shall dwell in the land that I gave to your fathers; you shall be My people, and I will be your God" (Eze. 36:25-28). Christ declared, "He who hears My word and believes in Him who sent Me has everlasting life, and shall not come into judgment, but has passed from death into life" (John 5:24).

It is exciting to live in the time of the investigative judgment, for it takes place just before the return of Jesus. The judgment reveals God's righteousness in saving those who have accepted His atonement. Thus it answers the questions raised by Satan.

The saints rejoice in the time of judgment, for it vindicates them! They have received the robe of Christ's righteousness and have lived by His power! Let us join in proclaiming that "the hour of His judgment has come"—a final phase in the plan of salvation that ushers in the Second Coming and the new earth.

---

* The Daniel and Revelation Committee of the General Conference of Seventh-day Adventists has dealt with the question of the cleansing of the heavenly sanctuary that began in heaven in 1844. The topic is too large to cover in the allotted space in this chapter. For a comprehensive summary of the committee's findings, see Frank B. Holbrook, *The Atoning Priesthood of Jesus Christ* (Adventist Theological Society Publications, 1996).

Chapter 8

Such a Cloud of Witnesses and the Second Coming

HAVE YOU ever attempted to relate to a noncommunicative person? Quickly you discovered that you never knew what they were thinking or planning. Perhaps you thought you were going out to dinner at the café next door and ended up at a five-star restaurant downtown (and felt underdressed)! Maybe you started on what you assumed was a shopping expedition at the mall, only to end up on a trip to a foreign country. A bit frustrating? Of course! Good relationships thrive on good communication.

As we have seen, Christianity is also a relationship—a relationship with lots of communication from God. God wants us to know about Him because He longs to fellowship with us. He does not seek to leave us in the dark—that is disruptive to all relationships. Instead, He wants to tell us about who He is and what He is doing in the future, because He would like us to take part in His plans. Amos assures us that God does nothing without revealing His plans to the prophets (Amos 3:7). God's overarching plan is for His people to preach the gospel of His soon coming kingdom in all the world because He wants to make sure that everyone has received an invitation to join in the wedding feast to take place at His second coming.

God has always operated this way throughout history. He has sent His messengers to invite His people and the world to prepare to join Him in special events. For example, He used Noah to invite people to seek safety in the ark (2 Peter 2:5).

God called Abraham out of Ur of the Chaldees and made from Him a great nation in order that "the nations of the earth" should "be blessed in him" (Gen. 18:18, 19). Through Abraham would come the Messiah and the people who would keep the hope of the Messiah alive in the world.

Caleb and Joshua received the task of encouraging Israel to move forward by faith into the Promised Land. At Kadesh-barnea Moses assigned 12 spies the task of examining the land of Canaan. Of the 12, only Caleb and Joshua voted to accept the word of the Lord and move forward. The vote of the other 10 sent Israel back into the wilderness for 40 years.

John the Baptist was the messenger prophesied by Isaiah to proclaim the coming of the Messiah (Isa. 40:3). The Baptist prepared a people to accept the coming Messiah by turning "many of the children of Israel to the Lord their God" (Luke 1:16, 17). He witnessed to Christ, saying, "Behold! The Lamb of God who takes away the sin of the world!" (John 1:29).

What Kind of Witnesses?

What characteristic was decisive for God when He chose Noah, Abraham, Caleb, Joshua, John the Baptist, and many others—"so great a cloud of witnesses" (Heb. 12:1)—to carry His special message to their generation? Hebrews 11 enumerates many of God's chosen messengers and emphasizes that they successfully carried out God's will for their lives because they responded to Him in faith. Not only did each of them preach a message of faith in God, they also lived by faith, a faith that implied the Second Coming (Heb. 10:37, 38). Although they did not always live to see the things God promised them, their faith gave them assurance that He would fulfill His promises and warnings (Heb. 11:10, 13, 39).

"By faith Noah . . . prepared an ark for the saving of his household, by which he . . . became heir of the righteousness which is according to faith" (Heb. 11:7). Noah received a message for his generation warning of the earth's impending destruction by a worldwide flood. It summoned humanity to depart from their idolatrous and self-serving ways and worship the true God. Salvation awaited all those who desired to enter the ark.

Put yourself in Noah's place, and try to understand the faith it required to fulfill God's call. The human race had never known a destructive flood. People were happy with their evil ways, with their "designer god" who allowed them to live in sin. The God

THE CERTAINTY OF THE SECOND COMING

of heaven, however, asked Noah to commit his resources and 120 of the best years of his life to a cause that was not only unpopular, but that seemed foolish in the eyes of those around him.

The scientists from the best universities of his time made it clear that rain was out of the question. The most popular and prestigious theologians also clarified the issue—a god of love would not destroy the creatures whom he had created! The scholars condemned Noah "because he would not be turned from his purpose by reasonings and theories of men. It was true that Noah could not controvert their philosophies, or refute the claims of science so called; but he could proclaim the word of God; for he knew it contained the infinite wisdom of the Creator, and, as he sounded it everywhere, it lost none of its force and reality because men of the world treated him with ridicule and contempt" (*Signs of the Times,* Apr. 18, 1895). Noah lived by faith in the word of God.

"By faith Abraham obeyed when he was called to go out to the place which he would receive as an inheritance. . . . By faith he dwelt in . . . a foreign country, dwelling in tents. . . . By faith Abraham, when he was tested, offered up Isaac . . . of whom it was said, 'In Isaac your seed shall be called,' concluding that God was able to raise him up, even from the dead" (Heb. 11:8-19).

No reasonable evangelistic committee would have accepted God's request for Abraham to leave family and friends and the cultural metropolis of Ur of the Chaldees. The opportunities for evangelism were certainly much greater at one of the economic crossroads of the world than they would be in the sparsely populated land of Canaan. But it was not Abraham's place to question God's call. By faith, he went out without the least outward assurance that God would fulfill His promise (*Patriarchs and Prophets,* p. 126).

The divine command to sacrifice his son Isaac was even more unreasonable. It seemed totally contrary to God's character and to His promise and would only associate Abraham with pagans and their child sacrifices, certainly not a very good way to represent God in the land of Canaan. Furthermore, some might see Abraham as a murderer. How could he ever face Sarah, or the rest of his household? "By faith Abraham . . . offered up Isaac." Abraham lived by faith in the word of God.

Caleb and Joshua also operated by faith when they challenged Israel to obey the word of the Lord to depart from Kadesh-barnea and invade the land of Canaan. From a human military standpoint the task was impossible. Israel was untrained and unarmed. The Caananites were well prepared for battle. They had the latest military techniques, the best weapons, and they lived in well-fortified cities. No general in His right mind would take a nomadic tribe into such potential slaughter. But Caleb and Joshua heeded the voice of God, and urged Israel to seize the land under God's blessing (Num. 14:7-9, 24, 30).

Also by faith they led Israel against Jericho. "By faith the walls of Jericho fell down after they were encircled for seven days" (Heb. 11:30). Imagine the trust and loyalty to God of those willing to capture the city by "senselessly" marching around it for seven days. Caleb and Joshua lived by faith in the word of God.

Had Hebrews 11 mentioned New Testament heroes of faith, the name of John the Baptist would have been there. It is possible that verse 37 alludes to him—"They wandered about in sheepskins and goatskins, being destitute." Many occasions in John's life could have sparked doubt, "but the Baptist did not surrender his faith in Christ" (*The Desire of Ages,* p. 216). John lived by faith in the word of God.

What Is Faith?

Faith played a key role in the lives and preaching of each messenger of God. Since faith had such an important factor, it is vital for us to understand what faith is.

We could analyze faith from a human standpoint to develop a definition. In our attempt to discover its nature, we could explore the faith of a scientist in his hypotheses, of a historian in his thesis, or of a banker in granting a mortgage.

Bankers do a careful analysis before they approve a loan, studying such factors as the applicant's age, sex, health, payment history on prior loans, net worth, and income. They test each criteria by current banking experience. The banking official may conclude, based upon the combination of such factors, that a 99.8 percent chance exists that the person will repay the loan as agreed. Using such information, and relying upon their skills as an analyst, the bankers have enough "faith" to be willing to grant the loan.

Historians analyze their sources, determining their probable reliability and the way that they relate with other pieces of data such as that provided by archaeology, dating, climatology, etc. After synthesizing the data, they interpret them in terms of their own historical frame of reference and worldview. Based upon such synthesis and interpretation, historians make a "faith" statement regarding the reality and significance of some event.

Scientists likewise collect data in the laboratory, synthesize it, and then interpret it according to "known" facts. They then develop a hypothesis, a "faith" statement, on how new pieces of data will fit into the current scientific model.

Each example grounds faith upon the evidence of the "data" collected and interpreted by the particular model of the banker, historian, or scientist. The interpretation then leads to a conclusion, or "faith" statement. Such a method of defining faith uses a humanistic, or people-centered, approach to knowledge. We have already seen in chapter 6 that it is not our job to develop a designer concept of salvation. Salvation is God's gift rather than our creation. If we are to receive salvation by faith, then we must allow God the privilege of defining that faith. The humanistic approach to faith places our confidence upon the foundation of human ingenuity, upon our ability to collect, synthesize, and interpret the "evidence."

The biblical concept of faith is quite distinct, however. Faith is not a human creation, but rather the gift of God that rests upon divine power instead of human achievement (Eph. 2:8; 1 Cor. 2:5). "Faith that enables us to receive God's gifts is itself a gift" (*Education,* p. 253). "No man can create faith. The Spirit operating upon and enlightening the human mind, creates faith in God. In the Scriptures faith is stated to be the gift of God, powerful unto salvation, enlightening the hearts of those who search for truth as for hidden treasure" (*The Seventh-day Adventist Bible Commentary,* Ellen G. White Comments, vol. 7, p. 940).

Faith is itself the ground, the assurance, the conviction of things not seen (Heb. 11:1). It is the eye that sees, the ear that hears (*The Spirit of Prophecy,* vol. 3, p. 182). As the basis of knowledge, it is through faith that we understand (Heb. 11:3). And as the key of knowledge (*Education,* p. 24; *The Desire of Ages,* p. 139), it enables us to discern between truth and error (*Selected Messages,* book 2, p. 58). The humanistic approach states that we must find a foundation, the criteria for faith, whereas the biblical approach states that faith *is* the foundation, the criteria.

According to the Bible, faith does not come by our humanistic analysis of the data of the natural world, but by hearing the Word of God (Rom. 10:17). "Our assurance and evidence [for faith] is God's word" (*ibid.,* book 2, p. 243). The attempt to found our faith in the Bible as the Word of God upon data interpreted through reason is to doubt that which God has already declared. It is similar to the temptation Satan offered Christ in the wilderness, namely, to doubt His Sonship after the Word of God had already affirmed it. "Genuine faith has its foundation in the promises and provisions of the Scriptures" (*The Desire of Ages,* p. 126; cf. *Early Writings,* p. 72; *Gospel Workers,* p. 260).

To base our faith in Scripture upon the description of a historian or a geologist indicates that we have not yet come to biblical faith. "In order to have true, abiding faith in Christ, we must know Him as He is represented in the word" (*Fundamentals of Christian Education,* p. 433). The Spirit and the Word work together. "The spirit operating upon and enlightening the human mind, creates faith in God" (*The Seventh-day Adventist Bible Commentary,* Ellen G. White Comments, vol. 7, p. 940). Biblical faith comes through the Word under the work of the Spirit.

The faith that God gives us is powerful. Reinforcing and building upon itself, it is contagious, for we can share it with others.

Danger in Doubt

The context of the faith chapter (Hebrews 11) also contains a warning: "Do not cast away your confidence" (Heb. 10:35). Doubt is also powerful, building upon itself. And it is contagious, for it can be caught by others.

THE CERTAINTY OF THE SECOND COMING

The contemporary humanistic way of thinking begins with doubt. People question everything in order to determine what is truth. That which survives the fire of cross-examination they accept as rock-solid knowledge, something on which to place one's faith. Some apply the same method to the Bible, calling everything into question from a scientific, historical, psychological, philosophical, archaeological, or geological perspective in order to determine what is truth in the Bible. The very method itself starts with and builds upon doubt in the veracity of Scripture. Christ asked, "When the Son of Man comes, will He really find faith on the earth?" (Luke 18:8).

Ellen White raises questions about humanistic methods that start with a presupposition of doubt: "God has permitted a flood of light to be poured upon the world in both science and art; but when professedly scientific men treat upon these subjects from a merely human point of view, they will assuredly come to wrong conclusions. It may be innocent to speculate beyond what God's word has revealed, if our theories do not contradict facts found in the Scriptures; but those who leave the word of God, and seek to account for His created works upon scientific principles, are drifting without chart or compass upon an unknown ocean. The greatest minds, if not guided by the word of God in their research, become bewildered in their attempts to trace the relations of science and revelation. Because the Creator and His works are so far beyond their comprehension that they are unable to explain them by natural laws, they regard Bible history as unreliable. Those who doubt the reliability of the records of the Old and New Testaments, will be led to go a step further, and doubt the existence of God; and then, having lost their anchor, they are left to beat about upon the rocks of infidelity" (*Patriarchs and Prophets,* p. 113).

It would be nice if we could go back and rewrite biblical history. It would start like this: "By faith, when confronted by the serpent in the tree in the garden of Eden, Eve was victorious through her allegiance to the Word of God. She responded to Satan, 'It is written, you shall not eat of the tree of the knowledge of good and evil, for in the day that you eat of it, you shall surely die.'" Instead, Eve responded with methodological doubt in the word of God. By also starting with doubt, the contemporary process of learning continues the same method Eve used in the garden.

The antediluvians employed the same approach to argue against Noah. Science said that it would not rain, and theology (philosophy) claimed that a God of love would not destroy the creatures of His creation.

Israel followed the same procedure of doubt in the word of God when it responded to Caleb and Joshua. God cannot possibly ask us to go up against the Caananites, they argued. It is unreasonable for Him even to consider it. Far better it would have been for us if we had died in Egypt or in the wilderness (Deut. 9:23).

"And this is the object which Satan seeks to accomplish. There is nothing that he desires more than to destroy confidence in God and in His word. Satan stands at the head of the great army of doubters. . . . It is becoming fashionable to doubt. There are many who seem to feel that it is a virtue to stand on the side of unbelief, skepticism, and infidelity. But underneath an appearance of candor and humility, it will be found that such persons are actuated by self-confidence and pride. It is a terrible thing to lose faith in God or in His word. Unbelief strengthens as it is encouraged. There is danger in even once giving expression to doubt; a seed is sown which produces a harvest of its kind. Satan will nourish the crop every moment. Those who allow themselves to talk of their doubts will find them constantly becoming more confirmed. God will never remove every occasion for doubt. He will never work a miracle to remove unbelief when He has given sufficient evidence for faith" (*The Spirit of Prophecy,* vol. 4, p. 349).

The following brief quotations will summarize Ellen White's concern about the insidious nature of doubt:

"Satan is the parent of unbelief, murmuring, and rebellion" (*The Seventh-day Adventist Bible Commentary,* Ellen G. White Comments, vol. 1, p. 1087). "It is a sin to doubt" (*Selected Messages,* book 3, p. 149). "Disguise it as they may, the real cause of doubt and skepticism, in most cases, is the love of sin" (*Steps to Christ,* p. 111). "Those who love sin will turn away from the Bible, will love to doubt, and will become reckless in principle" (*Testimonies,* vol. 1, p. 441).

"If we talk doubt, and encourage doubt, we shall have abundant doubt; for Satan will help us in this kind of work" (*Signs of the Times,* May 2, 1895, p. 4). "Jesus never praised unbelief; He never commended doubts" (*Testimonies,* vol. 4, p. 233). "Sow not one expression of doubt" (*Review and Herald,* Feb. 6, 1894, p. 9).

"If you choose to open the door to the suggestions of the evil one, your mind will be filled with distrust and rebellious questioning. You may talk out your feelings, but every doubt you utter is a seed that will germinate and bear fruit in another's life, and it will be impossible to counteract the influence of your words" (*Our High Calling,* p. 319). "We do not want to speak one word of doubt and thus praise the devil for his wonderful power to keep you in subjection" (*Mind, Character, and Personality,* vol. 2, p. 675).

"I was shown that those who are troubled with doubts and infidelity should not go out to labor for others. That which is in the mind must flow out, and they realize not the effect of a hint or the smallest doubt expressed. Satan makes it a barbed arrow. It acts like a slow poison, which, before the victim is made sensible of his danger, affects the whole system, undermines a good constitution, and finally causes death. It is just so with the poison of doubt and unbelief of Scripture facts. One who has influence suggests to others that which Satan has suggested to him, that one scripture contradicts another; and thus, in a very wise manner, as though he had found out some wonderful mystery which had been hid from believers and the holy in every age of the world, he casts midnight darkness into other minds. They lose the relish they once had for the truth and become infidels. All this is the work of a few words spoken, which had a hidden power because they seemed involved in mystery" (*Testimonies,* vol. 1, p. 377).

At the end of the parable of the rich man and Lazarus, Christ comes to a decisive conclusion: If we will not hear Moses and the prophets, neither will we be persuaded though one rise from the dead! (Luke 16:31).

Humanism Versus the Word of God

A major difference exists between the way the messengers of God discussed above believed, and those who rejected the Word of God. Eve, the antediluvians, and Israel at Kadesh-barnea wished to found their beliefs humanistically—upon the evidences of their senses, logic, philosophy, observation. They wanted a reasonable belief in a "designer god." Instead of founding their human study upon the Word of God, they sought to test the Word of God by their human study. By contrast, Noah, Abraham, Caleb, Joshua, John, and Christ accepted the Word of God by faith—they had a belief based upon an "It is written," and therefore accepted the God who revealed Himself instead of the idols of human making.

Paul warns: "As you therefore have received Christ Jesus the Lord, so walk in Him, rooted and built up in Him and established in the faith. . . . Beware lest anyone cheat you through philosophy and empty deceit, according to the tradition of men, according to the basic principles of the world, and not according to Christ" (Col. 2:6-8).

Suppose that the Redskins football team received an invitation to play a game with the Red Sox baseball team. How could the two teams find common ground in the rules of the two different games to be able to play at all? Which ball would they use? Which stadium would accommodate them? Who would umpire the game? What rules would they use? The games are so different that they could not be blended. A bat on the football field would be out of place. At the same time, a football on a baseball field would be so awkward that the game would fall apart. One team could ask the other to join them in their ballpark for their ball game, but they could not compromise in such a way as to blend the two games.

So Noah, Caleb and Joshua, John the Baptist, and Christ all worked on completely different sets of principles than their contemporaries. Abraham's relatives could not even understand his response to God's call. Noah could not controvert the arguments of the scientists on their ground. But they could invite their contemporaries to join them in their ballpark, and play their ball game, based upon their rules of faith rather than the humanistic principles of the world. They proclaimed the gospel, and it lost none of its power because they did not compromise with the humanism of their age. So as Christians living at the end of time, we will also live by faith in God's Word instead of by the humanism of our age.

God is calling not only for conversion of the heart, but also conversion of the mind. He would like us to think biblically rather than humanistically. Just as Noah called the people of his time into his ark, so God is looking for us to be His messengers today to preach His Word, summoning others to prepare to meet Him at His second coming. Choose you this day whom you will serve. God has an open invitation for you to join Him in His ball game.

Chapter 9

The Witness of the Remnant and the Second Coming

I WOULD LIKE to tell you about a personal and close friend of mine. We live almost at opposite ends of the continent, meaning that we do not have opportunity to see each other very often. However, we look forward to those rare occasions, and cherish each moment we have together. I have never seen him without a smile. Even on bad hair days (if men have such) he talks about his difficulties with an exuberant sense that everything is all right because it is in God's hands. He is energetic, yet quiet mannered. His disposition is even, and he is pleasant to be around. My friend always has new projects and horizons to explore, because he is on the cutting edge of his discipline. But what I like about him the most is his interest in people. I suspect his students love him, especially since I have seen him slide in next to a financially disadvantaged student in the cafeteria line and quietly pick up the student's charge on his own account.

Suppose I decided that my friend is not really interested in people—that he cares about only what he can get out of them. That is why he is such a nice guy. My suspicions would soon begin to affect our relationship. Not so much from his end—he would still be the same caring, outgoing individual—but from mine. Our relationship would alter because I would begin to change toward him. Questioning his actions, I would be cautious in opening up to him. Our relationship would become strained, if not broken. A healthy relationship between us depends upon my acknowledging and accepting him for who he is.

A healthy relationship with God also involves our accepting Him for who He is. If I were to deny essential aspects of God's character, it would distort, if not sever, my relationship with

Him. Not because God has withdrawn His loving outstretched arms, but because I no longer see Him as having those arms outstretched in my direction.

How would it affect my relationship with God if I were to decide that He is not loving and compassionate, but hateful and avenging? Suppose I said that the Bible is not His Word and therefore not His self-revelation? That it is only a collection of reflections by religiously talented people about their encounter with God? What if I were to say, "God, I do not believe that You created me, that You sent Your Son to die as an atonement for my sins, that You are coming back the second time to take home with You those who have accepted Your Son as their Saviour"? Or what if I challenged, "God, I am not Your servant, but Your equal"? Suppose I did not accept that God will eventually destroy the wicked at the end of the millennium, or that He is interested in whether human beings keep His law.

If I affirmed any of the above concepts, I would be denying portions of the character of the God who has revealed Himself. In spite of His outstretched arms of love, I would be putting myself outside the reach of His love. And if I tried to worship the limited God I imagined, I would be embracing an idol, a "designer god," rather than the true God of the universe. God cannot take home with Him those attached to their idols, for it is not possible to have a unique, intimate relationship with those who devote themselves to someone or something else. We must give God our complete allegiance if we are to enter a full relationship with Him.

No wonder Paul was so concerned about those who "profess" to know God. The apostle admonished Titus to use sound doctrine to exhort and convict those who contradict the truth, in the process subverting whole households (Titus 1:8-11, 16; 2:1). The Bible uses the word "truth" more than 200 times. In most cases it refers to God or to His Word. "Sanctify them by Your truth. Your word is truth" (John 17:17).

We may know the truth by correctly interpreting God's Word (2 Tim. 2:15). We twist the Word of God at the risk of our own destruction (2 Peter 2:16). Those who do not desire truth will soon follow teachers promoting fables (2 Tim. 4:3, 4).

Many will reject or drift away from truth before the second coming of Christ. Satan will oppose and exalt himself above God, even claiming to be God. Those who accept him in place of truth will condemn themselves. Our salvation comes through sanctification by the Spirit and belief in the truth (2 Thess. 2:1-16).

Pagan Interpretations

Apostasy started even at the time of the apostles, and occurred even more rapidly after their death. The church attempted to accommodate itself to a hostile pagan world to survive and gain converts. It adopted the current methods of interpreting literature and employed contemporary philosophical thinking. Origen, for example, was a biblical scholar in the second century A.D. working out of the city of Alexandria. Pagan scholars of the time used the allegorical method of interpretation on centuries-old historical traditions. They emphasized the spiritual rather than the literal meaning of the text. Origen applied the method to the study of the Bible. Although he usually sought a literal interpretation of the text, when the teaching of the Bible went against the philosophy of his age he applied a spiritual meaning so that the Bible would not be "unreasonable" to contemporary pagans. Only in that way, he thought, could he win them to Christianity.

Ellen White notes that "the advancing centuries witnessed a constant increase of error in the doctrines put forth from Rome. Even before the establishment of the papacy the teachings of heathen philosophers had received attention and exerted an influence in the church. Many who professed conversion still clung to the tenets of their pagan philosophy, and not only continued its study themselves, but urged it upon others as a means of extending their influence among the heathen. Serious errors were thus introduced into the Christian faith. Prominent among these was the belief in man's natural immortality and his consciousness in death. This doctrine laid the foundation upon which Rome established the invocation of saints and the adoration of the Virgin Mary. From this sprang also the heresy of eternal torment for the finally impenitent, which was early incorporated into the papal faith" (*The Great Controversy*, p. 58).

The church had great success in its attempt to win the pagan world to Christianity. The result was that paganism walked right into the church and was "baptized." Pagan Sunday worship substituted itself for God's Sabbath; the concept of a natural immortality of the soul infiltrated biblical teaching on death, and infant baptism and sprinkling took the place of adult baptism by immersion. Christians began to assume that access to God worked the same way that ordinary people needed to reach the elite—through intermediaries. They sought God through priests and saints instead of directly approaching Him. Salvation was by faith and deeds instead of by faith alone. One could atone for sin through the purchase of a pardon rather than by submission to Jesus Christ. The Bible was no longer the authority for theology and life. Tradition, church councils, philosophy, and human reason began to supplement and even replace it.

As time went on, the Bible took on a diminishing role. The laity had virtually no access to it. Even the clergy seldom had opportunity to read it. Tradition, church councils, and philosophy took on larger roles. With the Bible no longer as guide, abuse became rampant in the church. Ellen White describes the selling of indulgences at the time of Luther: "Tetzel sets up his traffic in the church, and ascending the pulpit, he with great vehemence extols indulgences as the most precious gifts of God. 'Draw near,' he cries, 'and I will give you letters, duly sealed, by which the sins you hereafter desire to commit shall be all forgiven you.' 'Even repentance is not indispensable.' 'But more than all this, indulgences save not only the living but the dead.' 'The very moment that the money clinks against the bottom of this chest, the soul escapes from purgatory, and flies to Heaven'" (*Signs of the Times*, June 14, 1883).

The Reformation and the Word of God

The church had gained power over every aspect of life, including government. Kings and magistrates were at the beck and call and the mercy of the church. Education also fell under its tight control. Sometimes to study, translate, and disseminate the

THE WITNESS OF THE REMNANT

Scriptures put one's life at risk. In spite of the tight power of the church, the Protestant Reformers in many countries stepped out in courage and faith. The intensity of the battle and the loyalty of the Reformers to the authority of the Bible as the Word of God appears in the following references from *The Great Controversy:* At his trial, Jerome declared: "'Prove to me from the Holy Writings that I am in error, . . . and I will abjure it.'

"'The Holy Writings!' exclaimed one of his tempters, 'is everything then to be judged by them? Who can understand them till the church has interpreted them?'

"'Are the traditions of men more worthy of faith than the gospel of our Saviour?' replied Jerome. 'Paul did not exhort those to whom he wrote to listen to the traditions of men, but said, "Search the Scriptures."'

"'Heretic!' was the response, 'I repent having pleaded so long with you. I see that you are urged on by the devil'" (p. 114).

Olaf Petri of Sweden "declared that the teachings of the Fathers are to be received only when in accordance with the Scriptures; that the essential doctrines of the faith are presented in the Bible in a clear and simple manner, so that all men may understand them. . . . He showed that the decrees of the church are of no authority when in opposition to the commands of God, and maintained the great Protestant principle that 'the Bible and the Bible only' is the rule of faith and practice" (p. 243).

"Luther saw the danger of exalting human theories above the Word of God. He fearlessly attacked the speculative infidelity of the schoolmen and opposed the philosophy and theology which had so long held a controlling influence upon the people. He denounced such studies as not only worthless but pernicious, and sought to turn the minds of his hearers from the sophistries of philosophers and theologians to the eternal truths set forth by prophets and apostles" (p. 126).

"Fearlessly did Luther defend the gospel from the attacks which came from every quarter. The Word of God proved itself a weapon mighty in every conflict. With that word he warred against the usurped authority of the pope, and the rationalistic philosophy of the schoolmen, while he stood firm as a rock against

THE CERTAINTY OF THE SECOND COMING

the fanaticism that sought to ally itself with the Reformation.

"Each of these opposing elements was in its own way setting aside the Holy Scriptures and exalting human wisdom as the source of religious truth and knowledge. Rationalism idolizes reason and makes this the criterion for religion. Romanism, claiming for her sovereign pontiff an inspiration descended in unbroken line from the apostles, and unchangeable through all time, gives ample opportunity for every species of extravagance and corruption to be concealed under the sanctity of the apostolic commission. The inspiration claimed by Münzer and his associates proceeded from no higher source than the vagaries of the imagination, and its influence was subversive of all authority, human or divine. True Christianity receives the Word of God as the great treasure house of inspired truth and the test of all inspiration" (p. 193).

The protest of the princes at the Diet of Spires, at the risk of losing their positions, and even their lives, also upheld the authority of Scripture. "'There is no sure doctrine but such as is conformable to the Word of God. . . . The Lord forbids the teaching of any other doctrine. . . . The Holy Scriptures ought to be explained by other and clearer texts; . . . this Holy Book is, in all things necessary for the Christian, easy of understanding, and calculated to scatter the darkness. We are resolved, with the grace of God, to maintain the pure and exclusive preaching of His only Word, such as it is contained in the biblical books of the Old and New Testaments, without adding anything thereto that may be contrary to it. This Word is the only truth; it is the sure rule of all doctrine and of all life, and can never fail or deceive us. He who builds on this foundation shall stand against all the powers of hell, while all the human vanities that are set up against it shall fall before the face of God.'. . . 'The principles contained in this celebrated Protest . . . constitute the very essence of Protestantism'" (p. 203).

Zwingli also presented the Word of God as the only infallible authority. He stated that he was not introducing a new method but the old approach employed by the church in earlier and purer times. "The more he searched the Scriptures, the clearer appeared the contrast between their truths and the heresies of Rome. He submitted himself to the Bible as the Word of God, the only sufficient, infallible rule. He saw that it must be its own interpreter" (p. 173).

During several centuries and in many countries, Reformers proclaimed the need to return to the Bible alone. While many differences existed among the Reformers themselves, they were unified on several points: (1) the Bible alone under the Holy Spirit is the foundation of our lives and thinking; (2) the Bible is not to have any other system imposed upon it, whether it be ecclesiastical, philosophical, empirical, or existential; (3) the Bible is to be its own interpreter. That meant not only that one portion of the Bible was understood in the context of the whole of Scripture, but that no external method (such as the allegorical method) was to be imposed upon Scripture.

The Enlightenment and the Word of God

The era of the Enlightenment followed the period of the Reformation. The Enlightenment emphasized the autonomy of humanity from any church authority, and from divine authority as expressed in the Bible. Humanity had come of age! No longer under the tutelage of God or church, human beings were free to determine their own truth (rather than receiving it from God), and they were mature enough to make their own way in the world. If God did exist, and if the Bible was His Word, that would be decided on the basis of human principles (a philosophy called humanism). Whatever God was, it was necessary for Him to pass the test of human reason and sense experience. Philosophy, history, and particularly science became the authorities founded upon human reason and observation. It was within this historical context that the contemporary criteria for knowledge developed. Truth became what we could test in the laboratory, observe in the geological column, and verify from the records of history. God's Word took second place to liberal education.

The historical-critical method for the study of the Bible came out of the era of the Enlightenment. It imposes the criteria of the Enlightenment upon the Bible, just as earlier methods such as the allegorical approach, overlaid other alien philosophical presuppositions on Scripture. The Bible no longer could be its own interpreter. The historical-critical method was basically the application of the principles of humanism to Bible study. Scholars approached the Bible as one would any other piece of literature. No longer did they recognize its uniqueness as the Word of God. They viewed it as a piece of literature subject to the same forces that produced other bits of folk literature. Many regarded it not as a unity, but as separate pieces of literature that chronicle the evolutionary development of spirituality in humanity.

Ellen White was concerned about the effect of higher criticism upon faith in the Bible. "The warnings of the Word of God regarding the perils surrounding the Christian church belong to us today. As in the days of the apostles men tried by tradition and philosophy to destroy faith in the Scriptures, so today, by the pleasing sentiments of higher criticism, evolution, spiritualism, theosophy, and pantheism, the enemy of righteousness is seeking to lead souls into forbidden paths. To many the Bible is as a lamp without oil, because they have turned their minds into channels of speculative belief that bring misunderstanding and confusion. The work of higher criticism, in dissecting, conjecturing, reconstructing, is destroying faith in the Bible as a divine revelation. It is robbing God's Word of power to control, uplift, and inspire human lives" (*The Acts of the Apostles,* p. 474).

The Proclamation of the Everlasting Gospel

The era of the Enlightenment was the intellectual context into which God called the Adventist Church. He brought us out of churches that by and large had not yielded to the principles of the Enlightenment and that generally accepted the Protestant principle of *sola scriptura*. Our task was to finish what the Reformation had started—the complete return to the Word of God. It meant the proclamation of the "everlasting gospel"—the total message of God's Word for His people living in the last days. Among other things, it stressed two main truths not yet restored by the Reformation—"the hour of His judgment has come," and the call to "worship Him who made heaven and earth, the sea and springs of water" (Rev. 14:7). It was a message God wanted preached just before the second coming of Christ (verses 14-20).

The Judgment

As we saw in chapter 7, Christ went into the Most Holy Place of the heavenly sanctuary in 1844 to begin the investigative phase of the judgment that would take place just before the Second Coming. Because God will make judgment in their favor, it is good news for His people. Those who have by faith accepted the righteousness of God on their behalf will be prepared to participate in the Second Advent. Just as God has told us beforehand of His previous major actions on behalf of His people, so He also raised up a people to proclaim the prophecies of Daniel and Revelation relating to the time of the judgment. And just as God revealed Himself as working for Israel and then the whole human race at the cross, so God also desired to let us know the good news of what He was doing for us in the investigative judgment beginning in 1844. Thus the message of the first angel of Revelation 14: "Then I saw another angel flying in the midst of heaven, having the everlasting gospel to preach to those who dwell on the earth—to every nation, tribe, tongue, and people—saying with a loud voice, 'Fear God and give glory to Him, for the hour of His judgment has come'" (verses 6, 7).

Worship the Creator

The second aspect of the first angel's message is to "worship Him who made heaven and earth, the sea and springs of water" (verse 7). Just at the time when some began to question God's role and the manner of His creation, God fulfilled the prophecy that there would be a people who would accept and proclaim the biblical teaching on Creation. As we have seen in chapter 3, the acceptance of the biblical concept of six-day creation by the Word of God has major implications for our concept of the nature of God. If God either cannot or does not act in the way Genesis 1 and 2 report, then why should we expect Him to be similarly active at the cross, in the resurrection of Jesus Christ, in His service in the heavenly sanctuary, and at the Second Coming? Should the record of the creation of life on earth be uncertain, then it throws into even greater doubt the promise of the literal, visible Second Coming and the resurrection of the righteous dead. Furthermore, acceptance of God's action in Creation is a faith statement (Heb. 11:3) that comes by faith in the Word of God. Thus worshiping God as Creator has major implications for the certainty of the Second Coming. The proclamation that God is our Creator is vital just before Christ's return in order that there might be a people ready to meet their God.

What is the biblical manner of worshiping the Creator? In chapter 4 we studied the role of the Sabbath as a memorial of Creation. "Remember the Sabbath day, to keep it holy. . . . For in six days the Lord made the heavens and the earth, the sea, and all that is in them, and rested the seventh day. Therefore the Lord blessed the Sabbath day and hallowed it" (Ex. 20:8-11). The Sabbath is a sign of God's authority. Nothing in history, astronomy, psychology, or any other human discipline would call for the worship of God on the Sabbath. Thus the Sabbath is a unique demonstration of allegiance to Him and of living by faith in His Word. No wonder some would think to change times and laws (Dan. 7:25). If humanity could alter God's law and the day of worship He established, then they could call into question His nature and eventually seize authority into their own hands. It was therefore important that there would be a reemphasis on worship of the true God just before the Second Coming—"Those from among you shall build the old waste places; you shall raise up the foundations of many generations; and you shall be called the Repairer of the Breach, the Restorer of Streets to Dwell In. If you turn away your foot from the Sabbath, from doing your pleasure on My holy day, and call the Sabbath a delight, the holy day of the Lord honorable, and shall honor Him, not doing your own ways, nor finding your own pleasure, nor speaking your own words, then you shall delight yourself in the Lord" (Isa. 58:12-14).

The restoration of the true Sabbath in the last days is important, because, as we saw in chapter 4, the Sabbath symbolizes our entire relationship with God. It points to Him first of all as a personal deity who desires to fellowship with us. Second, it reminds us that He is our Creator, Sustainer, Saviour, and the one who holds our future in His hand. As His sign of authority and power to create, it is an indication of our willingness to live by faith in

Him rather than by our own power. And as a symbol of the new earth to come, it also has major implications for the Second Coming that ushers us into our heavenly home with Christ.

The messages of the second and third angels of Revelation 14 (Rev. 14:8-11) warn humanity to leave those systems that have not returned to the full teaching of Scripture about God, and to His true worship. It summons the human race to discard human-made idolatrous systems that tamper with divine law and create a designer god in humanity's own image. Those who continue in their idolatrous ways will face divine wrath.

The Patience of the Saints

Revelation 14 resembles a river with quiet pools and treacherous cataracts. As we move into verses 6 and 7, we begin to feel the power of the water. By the time we reach verses 8-11, we find ourselves in the narrows. The water is wild and rough, pummeling first of all against one side of the canyon wall and then the other. But as we reach the other side, all is calm and peaceful—the peace that comes from faith in Jesus Christ. "Here is the patience of the saints; here are those who keep the commandments of God and the faith of Jesus" (verse 12).

Those who are prepared to participate in the proclamation of the three angels' messages are those who keep God's commandments. They obey them not as the basis of their salvation, but as a result of it. Not in order to be saved, but because they are already saved and want nothing to come between them and their Saviour. Each has the "Father's name written on their foreheads" (verse 1). "These are the ones who were not defiled with women [false doctrine], for they are virgins. These are the ones who follow the Lamb wherever He goes" (verse 4). They do not "drink of the wine of the wrath" of the fornication of Babylon (false doctrine), nor do they worship "the beast and his image," or receive "his mark" on their forehead or hand (verses 8, 9). All "keep the commandments of God" (verse 12).

Furthermore, the saints cling to "the faith of Jesus" (verse 12). The faith of Jesus was not an elaborate philosophical, scientific, or historical system—it rested upon the Word of God, upon

THE CERTAINTY OF THE SECOND COMING

"It is written." Just as friendship depends upon accepting a person for who they are, so it is important that we know the "only true God"—that we acknowledge and accept Him (John 17:3) on the basis of the Word of God, His self-revelation (verse 17). "Beloved, now we are children of God; and it has not yet been revealed what we shall be, but we know that when He is revealed, we shall be like Him, for we shall see Him as He is. And everyone who has this hope in Him purifies himself, just as He is pure" (1 John 3:2, 3). If we worship an idol of our own making—a "designer god" instead of the only true God—we will not be like the God returning at the Second Coming, and therefore we will not be ready for Him. Idolatry distorts or destroys our relationship with God. Thus the preaching of the three angels' messages takes place in order to give people the opportunity to avoid false doctrine and idolatry. It provides them a chance to accept the God who has revealed Himself in Jesus Christ and the Scriptures so that we may enter a relationship with the "only true God." Each may partake of the faith chapter (Heb. 11) to respond in faith to God's Word as did Noah, Abraham, Caleb, Joshua, John, and Christ Himself.

Ellen White indicates that there will be a people who, as the prophets, apostles, and Reformers before them, are willing to stand for the Word of God. They will not destroy the Bible as the Word of God by forcing upon it alien philosophies or methods of interpretation. "God will have a people upon the earth to maintain the Bible, and the Bible only, as the standard of all doctrines and the basis of all reforms. The opinions of learned men, the deductions of science, the creeds or decisions of ecclesiastical councils, as numerous and discordant as are the churches which they represent, the voice of the majority—not one nor all of these should be regarded as evidence for or against any point of religious faith. Before accepting any doctrine or precept, we should demand a plain 'Thus saith the Lord' in its support" (*The Great Controversy*, p. 595).

God is calling you to join with His people in proclaiming the everlasting gospel in order that the world might know and accept Him for who He is—the "only true God."

Chapter 10   BY ROLAND R. HEGSTAD

Should Our Nineteenth-Century Prophetic Schema Be Revised?

NEARLY 50 years ago, four months out of college, I preached my first prophetic sermon. Titled "Freedom at the Crossroads," it leaned heavily on standard Adventist prophetic fare. From today's perspective it was a bit in advance of Uriah Smith but considerably behind a few Adventist scholars who are suggesting that we must revisit and revise the prophetic scenario our Adventist pioneers constructed in the 1800s. They are concerned that the end-time scenario framed in the context of late-nineteenth-century United States just doesn't seem to fit well into today's dominantly secular society.

❖ For one example: No national Sunday law seems in the offing, as in the late 1800s. In 1950, when I placed freedom at the crossroads, all states but Alaska had Sunday laws. Since then, 21 states have taken them off their books, and another 18 have pulled so many enforcement teeth from them that they couldn't chew pudding. Only a half-dozen states sporadically attempt to enforce them.

❖ For a second example: Since Pope John XXIII convened Vatican Council II in 1962, the Roman Catholic Church has radically altered its posture on religious liberty. The sixteenth-century monk Beza pretty well epitomized his church's historic stance, calling religious liberty a "diabolical doctrine, because it leaves every man to go to hell in his own way." (Sixteenth-century males seemed to assume that women had their own built-in road map and needed no male assistance!) Today the Catholic Church appears quite willing to permit us to go to hell without its help—in fact, has apologized for the assistance it gave many

THE CERTAINTY OF THE SECOND COMING

"heretical" saints. Pope John Paul II has forthrightly spoken out for religious freedom. His posture doesn't seem to square with our traditional interpretation of Revelation 13.

❖ A third example: In 1961 the United States Supreme Court ruled that Sunday laws were legal *only* if they had a pervasive secular purpose. And it's difficult today to conceive of our pervasively secular society persecuting a group of people who want to worship on Saturday.

In *Time* magazine, June 15, 1998, Charles Krauthammer points out that religion, once a conviction, is now just a taste. The result: "Where religion is trivialized," Krauthammer observes, "one is unlikely to find persecution. When it is believed that on your religion hangs the fate of your immortal soul, the Inquisition follows easily; when it is believed that religion is a breezy consumer preference, religious tolerance flourishes easily. After all, we don't persecute people for their taste in cars. Why for their taste in gods?"

Who can rationally argue that the Sabbath is likely to become a test of loyalty in this age of what psychiatrists are calling the "new indifference"?

I agree with my scholarly friends that we must revisit the books of Daniel and Revelation. We are 100 years down the prophetic highway to tomorrow beyond where our forebears got off. Certainly it's possible that their "present truth" scenarios might require a bit of amending for our day. A few actors may have to be recostumed and their scripts rewritten to accommodate an updated "present truth." After all, Ellen White told her contemporaries that "we have only the glimmerings of the rays of the light that is yet to come to us" (*Review and Herald,* June 3, 1890).

Let me now begin to focus on the scholarly conclusion that today's secular world just doesn't fit within our traditional end-time scenario. Then we'll examine the six paramount points in our pioneers' late-1800s' exposition of "present truth" to see whether it must, indeed, be revised, and finally, I'll suggest a few "present truths" that our pioneers didn't foresee.

The one element above all others that seems to demand our reappraisal of the prophetic schema of our pioneers is secularism—the change from the Judeo-Christian society of the 1800s to the secular, humanistically oriented world of today. Apart from the Muslim segment, much is atheist or agnostic—certainly secular and emphatically materialistic. Western Europe is a post-Christian continent, its great cathedrals emptied, its Reformation heritage forgotten.

As for the United States, two Supreme Court decisions epitomize our secularism. The first, its ruling in the 1961 Sunday law cases that affirmed the constitutionality of Sunday laws only if they had a pervasively secular purpose. The second: a recent decision that a Christmas display in the Pawtucket, Rhode Island, city hall was constitutional because it was flanked by a secular Santa and his reindeer! Lawyers know the decision as the "plastic reindeer rule."

Maybe we should praise the Lord for secularism. Its disciples have almost succeeded in eliminating Sunday laws from our society, something our forebears couldn't achieve in 100 years! And secularists are generally indifferent to religion. Admit it: it's difficult to conceive of the secularist getting excited about whether someone worships or doesn't worship, whatever the day! If secularists go to church at all—sometimes it just seems the expedient thing to do—they create a humanist Lord that they can respect rather than worship. The humanist Lord, you see, asks only that we be religious, not that we take up His cross and follow Him.

Let's face up to it: Our traditional prophetic reading of Daniel and Revelation doesn't seem relevant in our secular world.

So let's review the five paramount "signs of the times," or "present truths," that led our expositors of the late 1800s to believe in Christ's imminent return. If we're presuming to rewrite the script, we ought to be thorough in our review.

1. The National Reform Association

I have an old notebook filled with newspaper clippings about the National Reform Association, founded in 1863 by representatives of 11 Protestant denominations. The inscription on the inside cover reads: *"Presented by Mrs. E. G. White to Religious Liberty Department."* She wanted the Religious Liberty Department, and through it, the church, to comprehend the prophetic nature of

THE CERTAINTY OF THE SECOND COMING

the association's plans, which were "to promote needed reforms in the action of the government touching the Sabbath" and "to secure such an amendment to the Constitution of the United States as will declare the nation's allegiance to Jesus Christ and its acceptance of the moral laws of the Christian religion" (in Warren L. Johns, *Dateline Sunday,* pp. 69, 70).

Ellen White called its religious amendment a "plain, direct fulfillment of prophecy" (*Testimonies,* vol. 5, p. 719). Some of our ministers, however, didn't feel they should preach on such a matter. She responded: "May the Lord forgive our brethren for thus interpreting the very message for this time" (*ibid.,* p. 715). "There have been surprising indifference and inactivity in this time of peril. Truth, present truth, is what the people need" (*ibid.,* p. 719).

By 1888 the National Reform Association's goals seemed attainable. Senator H. W. Blair of New Hampshire introduced legislation for a national Sunday law. Adventist pioneer editor A. T. Jones spoke in opposition to the bill before a congressional committee. The Blair bill died in committee in 1888 and, reincarnated, perished again in 1889.

2. The second actor on stage in the prophetic scenario was the United States Supreme Court, which in the 1892 case *Church of the Holy Trinity v. United States,* unanimously declared the United States to be "a Christian nation." Adventists viewed the decision as a prophetic step toward the worship test of Revelation 13.

3. The third actor came on stage in 1889 in the person of the Catholic Congress, which, meeting in Baltimore, resolved to unite with Protestants to secure "proper Sunday observance." The 1800s were not a time of ecumenical bliss. Such Catholic-Protestant union in support of Sunday legislation fit right into the Adventist eschatology schema.

4. The fourth actor was the Catholic-dominated labor movement that in 1903 Ellen White linked with the implementation of the boycott predicted in Revelation 13 (see letter 26, 1903, in *Selected Messages,* book 2, pp. 142, 143). Mrs. White was undoubtedly aware of the implications of Pope Leo XIII's 1891 encyclical *Rerum Novarum,* which contains this key paragraph:

"Workingmen's associations [labor unions] . . . must pay special and chief attention to the duties of religion and morality, and social betterment should have this chiefly in view, for the foundation of social laws . . . [is] thus laid in religion."

In agreeing to cooperate with Protestants to secure "proper Sunday observance," the Congress in Baltimore was implementing the principles of Leo's encyclical. The Catholic Church later honored Baltimore's James Cardinal Gibbons as the "champion of the American worker." In 1908 Samuel Gompers, head of the American Federation of Labor, was able to announce that the union had done "as much [as], if not more than, any other organized body of men and women to enforce observance of the Sunday rest day."

5. The fifth actor was a miracle-working force called "spiritualism." You're familiar, I'm sure, with the Fox sisters and their communication with the spirit world. This movement, many Adventist pioneers concluded, added credence to the concept of the immortality of the soul in the minds of the general public and was setting the world up for the appearance of the counterfeit christ.

The message of "Christ our righteousness," introduced by A. T. Jones and E. J. Waggoner at the 1888 General Conference session in Minneapolis, seemed calculated to prepare our church for Christ's imminent return.

You have just seen on stage five of the most significant actors in the late-nineteenth-century end-time drama perceived by our Adventist pioneers. In addition, you've heard them speak their prophetic lines, which, some tell us, do not fit well in today's secular society. In evaluating this claim, let's see whether we can find the same, or similar, actors reciting comparable lines today. Lines that we might then describe as "present truth."

1. The National Reform Association

It's gone, of course. But it left grandchildren: the Christian Coalition, the American Coalition for Traditional Values, the Christian Voice, and a number of others that are in politics right up to their earlobes. But, granted, no Christian Right organization of any stature is promoting a national Sunday law. However, they are urging a religious amendment to the Constitution. And

THE CERTAINTY OF THE SECOND COMING

as Stan Moonyhan, a prominent evangelical, wrote in *Liberty*: "I sense the mood of my fellow evangelicals, and it scares the daylights out of me."

So the National Reform Association's bloodline continues. Secularism hasn't put a tourniquet on that. And keep your eyes on a couple good evangelical organizations: Focus on the Family and Promise Keepers. I know James Dobson and pray for the success of his emphasis on the family, but his views on separation of church and state concern me. And I applaud the objectives of Promise Keepers. Thank God again for men assuming spiritual leadership in their homes because of this movement. But an interesting new form of ecumenism seems to have its roots in this organization.

On this point I see little reason to revise our prophetic schema.

2. What about the Supreme Court? Without question its decisions have made it clear not only that we no longer live in a Christian nation, but also that we have affirmed our status as a secular state. (Of course, we had only to watch television to discover that.) Other decisions of the Court, however, seem precursors of trouble to come. For one thing, it has held that the state no longer must demonstrate a "compelling interest" to interfere with our religious liberty. Justice Antonin Scalia, author of that decision, said, "Religious liberty is a luxury we can no longer afford." Finally, the court has declared unconstitutional the Religious Freedom Act, which would have restored the "compelling interest" test. Also long on the books of the High Court has been a doctrine most recently restated in the 1972 case *Wisconsin v. Yoder*: "*Interests of the highest order can overbalance legitimate claims to the free exercise of religion.*"

What would constitute such "interests"? A nuclear crisis? Economic collapse? The crime that may make an evening stroll in our neighborhood an adventure? Surely anything that would jeopardize the stability or even the very existence of our nation. Somehow, this legal doctrine seems to fit all too well in the last pages of *The Great Controversy*.

3. What about Protestant/Catholic cooperation on Sunday laws, as in the 1880s? Not at this point, but in light of recent events and, in particular, a new encyclical, stay tuned. Ironically,

another Supreme Court decision has done more to drive Catholics and Protestants into each other's arms than the Christian nation decision of 1892. I refer to *Roe v. Wade.* Anyone tempted to rewrite the persecution scheme of Revelation 13 should study the temperament of those caught up in an issue of eternal consequence, as they view abortion at whatever stage and for whatever reason.

4. Labor unions/Sunday laws

For the past several decades labor unions have declined in membership and influence. But the consolidations of major companies have caused workers once again to seek security through unions. Recent headlines highlight scores of mergers, all seemingly followed by news of massive layoffs. As Ellen wrote: "Gigantic monopolies will be formed" (*Selected Messages,* book 2, p. 142). Previous governmental administrations took care of a number of them, but they're coming back with a vengeance. And emerging with them in much of the world is economic chaos, which, Ellen White said, ultimately would get blamed on those who honor the Sabbath and thus prevent a restoration to God's favor and "temporal prosperity" (see *The Great Controversy,* p. 590).

Are labor unions showing an interest in Sunday laws? On the world scene German labor unions have been promoting a Sunday law for the European Union. If you don't belong to the union, you don't work; and if you do belong, you rest on Sunday, as papal social/labor encyclicals direct. Just a "straw," to be sure; but one doesn't need to throw a log into the current to find which way it is flowing. A straw will do just as well.

Do we have any evidence that the objectives of the social/labor encyclicals are still influencing unions, especially the Sunday law issue here in the U.S.? A few years back George Meany, who achieved the merger of the American Federation of Labor and the Congress of Industrial Organizations, received the Lataere Medal, the highest award the Catholic Church can bestow on a layman, for forwarding the objectives of the socio/economic encyclicals.

Let's turn now to several subsequent encyclicals to see whether the labor/Sunday law mating continues.

1961: *Mater et Magistra* (Pope John XXIII): "We exhort, as it were, with the words of God Himself, all men, whether public officials, . . . or representatives of management and labor, that they observe this command of God . . . and of the Catholic Church" (p. 76).

1991: *Centesimus Annus* (John Paul II) calls for legal enforcement of "the . . . basic right to Sunday rest" (p. 6).

1998: *Dies Domini*. John Paul II's most recent encyclical attempts what no preceding encyclical has: Rather than simply claim that the Roman Catholic Church changed the Sabbath from Saturday to Sunday, *Dies Domini* offers an exhaustive biblical justification for Sunday observance. A justification with which Protestants can feel far more comfortable than with the former claim. Another barrier falls by the wayside, and another sign of the times goes up. The encyclical emphasizes the moral obligation of the state to enact legislation to facilitate the "Sabbath" obligation—and uses the Mass to forecast the soon return of Jesus Christ.

5. Spiritualism

Visited your psychic lately? Millions do daily. Or consult their horoscope. Twenty-four percent of Americans believe in reincarnation. Millions believe in communion with the spirit world.

Ruth Montgomery, the world's most published psychic, has reported receiving a testimony from Ellen White. On the morning after finishing *The Great Controversy*, which an Adventist layman had sent her, Ruth Montgomery claimed to receive the following message from her spirit guide: "The woman White who wrote the book you are reading is here and says, 'Please, please disregard what I wrote about communication with the living dead.'"

Of spiritualism Ellen wrote: "Here [in spiritualism] is a channel wholly devoted to [Satan], under his control, and he can make the world believe what he will" (*Spiritual Gifts*, vol. 1, p. 178).

It appears to me—secular age or not—that the signs our pioneers cited as "present truth" are alive and well today. Some, such as spiritualism, are not only far advanced over Ellen White's time but claim to be more in touch with her than some of us are. Further, I see reason to affirm that prophetic markers point to an impending test over worship. The scenario of our day has indeed changed, but we should have no difficulty in recognizing the lead actors on stage in our soon-to-be-twenty-first-century world.

In fact, I believe that down here, on the prophetic highway, we can observe a few new signs erected since our pioneers got off. Signs that may constitute present truth and thus add to our confidence in the soon return of our Lord.

Briefly, here are four that I believe warrant our consideration.

1. Humanity's ability to destroy our world, specifically with nuclear weapons. You may instinctively respond, "Well, aren't things better now with the dissolution of the Soviet Union?" No. Actually, we're in greater danger today for a number of reasons.

First, we have the breakdown of security and corresponding economic chaos in the states of the former Soviet Union. The militant Muslim world has factions seeking to buy bomb components by which to punish the Great Satan, as they call the United States. And now at least six nations have bombs and have or are developing the capability to deliver them. Within a decade a half-dozen unfriendly nations will join the list.

The second reason the danger is greater now is that nuclear by-products are contaminating the atmosphere, water, and soil, such as the leakage of dump sites in Siberia; the pollution of seawaters off Murmansk; and areas of contamination such as Chernobyl. I'll mention one American site: Hanford. The government examiner of nuclear sites is a close friend. I told him one day that it would be tragic if Hanford waste got into the Columbia. "It's there," he replied. "We've detected it in salmon even at the mouth of the river. And it's leaching through the soil surrounding Hanford." John the revelator spoke of God destroying them that destroy (or corrupt) the earth (Rev. 11:18).

2. Genetic manipulation. I make no blanket criticism of the term, for in some forms it offers healing. But I am sorely troubled by the cloning of living beings. Recently the Washington *Post* headlined the cloning of one cow into six. A week later another *Post* headline read: "Cloned Human Embryo Created, South Korean Researchers Say"—a claim subsequently denied. But because much of my theology takes into consideration the fallen nature of humanity, I'll predict, without fear of being a false prophet, that a scientist is going to clone himself someday soon. And we will have two modern Albert Einsteins. Or for a multimillion-dol-

lar payment, two Saddam Husseins. The prospects are appalling.

Sometimes I fear that we may be about to intrude on a prerogative of God Himself. Ellen White wrote: "If there was one sin above another which called for the destruction of the race by the flood, it was the base crime of amalgamation of man and beast which defaced the image of God, and caused confusion everywhere" (*Spiritual Gifts,* vol. 3, p. 64). Again: "Every species of animal which God had created were preserved in the ark. The confused species which God did not create, which were the result of amalgamation, were destroyed by the flood" (*ibid.,* p. 75).

I wish I could ask Ellen White what she saw in vision. With F. D. Nichol and others, I don't believe she viewed some part-human part-animal beings produced in the laboratories of those great intellects before the Flood. But *something* brought down the wrath of God upon the world, *something* that may cause God to say again: "Nothing that they propose to do will now be impossible for them. Come, let us go down . . . and destroy them that destroy [or corrupt] the earth." Our pioneers didn't see this sign—though some surely strained their eyes looking for new present truths.

3. The ecumenical movements of our day. Catholic-Protestant cooperation, as I've noted, owes much in the United States to *Roe v. Wade*, but worldwide, more to Vatican Council II and the initiatives of Pope John XXIII. It has not developed enough yet to push jointly for Sunday observance, but the courtship is warming, and the theology on which Protestants and Catholics can unite is in the 1998 encyclical *Dies Domini*. Most significant are not the formal ecumenical agencies of our day, such as the National and World Council of Churches, but that denomination-transcending movement called "charismatic," with its 500 million-plus members who major on signs and wonders.

I see in the charismatic movement a melding of ecumenism and spiritualism. It is not the Holy Spirit that is producing "holy laughter" in Toronto and people crawling about and barking like dogs elsewhere. When similar phenomena occurred in early Adventist history, Ellen White had no difficulty in discerning their origin. Further, she wrote of an end-time counterfeit revival in which "multitudes" would exalt that "God is working marvelously for them, when the work is that of another spirit" (*The Great Controversy*, p. 464). Then we have the evangelical/Catholic dialogue that has produced a document assuring us that the theological differences that sparked the Reformation have now been resolved. Pope John Paul II wants to retrace the steps of Abraham. Why? Because three major faiths—Christianity, Islam, and Judaism—revere the ancient patriarch. And the Vatican has been testing the reaction to an invitation for the leading figures of Protestantism to meet with the pope. Startling concessions are being made for the sake of unity.

4. Communication satellites. We have long held that the last sign to be fulfilled before Christ's return is the gospel to the world. Well, it's going, praise the Lord, and with unprecedented rapidity. If we really believe that it is the last prophecy awaiting completion, then we must view the means of achieving that end as itself prophetic. NET '98 should add an exclamation mark to that conclusion.

Some months ago I watched the evening sky. The sun was setting, and the moment was neither night nor day. Far in the northwest a light appeared, brighter than a second-magnitude star. Like a finger etching a message on some vast, purple-domed Belshazzar's hall, a satellite wrote its way across the heavens and vanished.

Some might have seen it and praised the gods who sit on movable thrones. Others—vessels of wine clutched in nerveless fingers—traced its silvery trail and divined, perhaps, that our world has shrunk to a global village. But few sense that One seated upon a throne high and lifted up is giving a final editing to all human achievements—One who has "appointed a day on which He will judge the world" (Acts 17:31).

A few years ago the O. J. Simpson trial captured the attention of much of the world. Satellites carried the courtroom scenes into the living room of my relatives in the Czech Republic. How long do you think it would take to reach the world with the testing truth of when (or whom) we should worship if global television featured a showcase trial of an Adventist leader? Especially if the prosecutor appeared to have nail marks in his hands . . .

Even now the World Wide Web has a site called the Nuremberg Files.

THE CERTAINTY OF THE SECOND COMING

It reads like a wanted poster. On it are the names of hundreds of doctors who perform abortions, their addresses, their license numbers, and even the names of their children. Those who have been assassinated are crossed off while those just wounded appear shaded in gray.

Enough said.

I think a review of our prophetic positions is a good thing. My research reconfirmed my convictions that the changes in our world since the late 1800s don't add up to a failed prophetic scenario. And events of the past half century reveal that a great church has been quietly growing in world esteem and in power, just as our Adventist pioneers anticipated. Some world political leaders credit Pope John Paul II with precipitating the downfall of the Soviet Union. I see no reason to believe that the test over when and whom we should worship shall be long delayed.

Catholic author Francois Mauriac once shared his vision of end-time with readers of *Look* magazine. His graphic word picture often comes to mind as I review *The Great Controversy*'s closing scenes:

"The day will come when the last terrified men will no longer question the nationality of their last Shepherd. Among the corpses and the rubble, it will scarcely matter whether he came from Europe or from America. They will press about his white robe, which will be the only light in the darkness of the end of time, and suddenly he will raise his hand and the heavens will open and he will point out to them the Sign of the Cross" (*Look,* Mar. 8, 1955, pp. 32, 33).

Isaiah too shared a vision of the earth:
"The earth is . . . defiled under its inhabitants,
Because they have transgressed the laws,
Changed the ordinance,
Broken the everlasting covenant.
Therefore the curse has devoured the earth,
And those who dwell in it are desolate. . . .
And few men are left" (Isa. 24:5, 6).

One wonders whether we'll be ready this time . . .

Chapter 11
The Certainty of the Second Coming

TAKE A MOMENT out of your busy schedule. Closing your eyes, ask yourself, How would my life be different if I did not have the hope of the Second Coming? Would it change the way I live day by day? Would I behave differently? Would I make different plans for the future? How would the death of a parent or a child affect me? Would it alter the way I think about myself?

Now, change the subject and ask, How would it alter God's life if there were no Second Coming? When God made plans to create humans on earth, He included a provision to deal with the possible entrance of sin into the world. From the time of humanity's fall into sin, God has been actively carrying out His plan of redemption. First, He promised a Saviour to Adam and Eve in the garden. Then He developed the sacrificial and Temple system to model the plan of salvation for our understanding. He commissioned Noah to rescue the antediluvians from destruction, and He unleashed the Flood so that all knowledge of Him would not vanish from the earth. Later He called Abraham as the father of the faithful to manifest His grace in the world. Centuries afterward He brought the children of Israel out of Egypt so that they could witness more effectively for Him. Through His prophets He continually renewed His promise of a Messiah to save us from our sins. Eventually He sent His own Son to live as we must, to die in our place, to be resurrected on our behalf, and to ascend into heaven to minister for us. All through history He has worked through prophets, apostles, and Reformers to keep faith alive on the earth. In 1844 He had His Son enter the Most Holy Place of the heavenly sanctuary to vindicate the saints before the universe.

All of these activities on our behalf converge on one point—the second coming of Christ. Were it not for what God has already done, we would have no certainty of the Second Coming. And were it not for the Second Coming, God would not have done all of these things. Thus the promise of the Second Coming profoundly altered God's own life.

Eliminating the Second Advent from the plan of salvation would be somewhat like a banquet meal without the dessert, a concerto without a finale, a hike without reaching the peak, an ice-cream cone without the ice cream, a pregnancy without a delivery. The Second Coming is the culmination of God's desire to bring us back into fellowship with Himself. It restores face-to-face communion between God and humanity.

A Major Biblical Theme

Although the phrase "second coming" does not appear in the Bible, it is nonetheless a major theme of the Bible, and Scripture refers to it in many different ways. Paul alludes to Christ's second coming (2 Tim. 4:8). Christ Himself said, "I will come again" (John 14:3), and Hebrews declares that Christ "will appear a second time" for salvation (Heb. 9:28).

While the Old Testament naturally emphasizes the First Advent, it does mention criteria that demand a Second Coming. "For I know that my Redeemer lives, and He shall stand at last on the earth; and after my skin is destroyed, this I know, that in my flesh I shall see God, whom I shall see for myself, and my eyes shall behold, and not another" (Job 19:25-27). The psalmist said: "Our God shall come, and shall not keep silent; a fire shall devour before Him, and it shall be very tempestuous all around Him" (Ps. 50:3; cf. Isa. 66:15, 16; Ps. 96:13). Jude 14 tells us that the patriarch Enoch preached that the Lord will come "with ten thousands of His saints."

The New Testament contains numerous references to the Second Coming. Christ Himself promised to return: "Let not your heart be troubled; you believe in God, believe also in Me. In My Father's house are many mansions; if it were not so, I would have told you. I go to prepare a place for you. And if I go and prepare a place for you, I will come again and receive you to Myself; that where I am, there you may be also" (John 14:1-3; cf. Luke 21:27-30; Rev. 22:7, 12, 20).

"Our Lord repeatedly referred to 'the coming of the Son of man' (Mt 24:27, 37, 39; cf. 16:27, 28; Mk 13:26; 14:62; Lk 9:26; etc.) and of His being 'revealed' (Lk 17:30). Paul speaks of 'the coming of our Lord Jesus Christ' (1 Th 5:23; etc.), or more simply of 'his coming' (2 Th 2:8; etc.) or 'his appearing' (2 Ti 4:8). James refers to 'the coming of the Lord' (Jas 5:7, 8), and Peter to the 'coming of our Lord Jesus Christ' (2 Pe 1:16) and the 'coming of the day of God' (ch 3:12). Throughout the NT, reference is made to 'that day' (Mt 7:22; 24:36; Lk 10:12; 21:34; 2 Ti 4:8; etc.), 'the day' (Rom 13:12; Heb 10:25; etc.), 'the day of our Lord' (1 Cor 1:8), 'the day of the Lord Jesus' (1 Cor 5:5; 2 Cor 1:14), and 'the day of Jesus Christ' (Php 1:6)" (*Seventh-day Adventist Bible Dictionary* [1979], p. 999).

"The usual NT terms for the 2d coming of Christ are *parousia,* 'presence,' 'outshining'; *epiphaneia,* 'appearance,' 'appearing'; and *apokalupsis,* 'revelation.' *Parousia* appears commonly in the papyri for the visit of an emperor or king. It is sometimes used to denote 'presence' as opposed to 'absence,' as in Php 2:12, but more commonly describes 'coming' as of Christ (2 Th 2:1), or of men (1 Cor 16:17). *Epiphaneia* occurs often in classical Greek to describe the glorious appearance of the pagan gods. In the NT it is used exclusively for the glorious 1st (2 Ti 1:10) and 2d (1 Ti 6:14; 2 Ti 4:1, 8; Tit 2:13) advents of the Lord Jesus. *Apokalupsis* is used of the 'appearing' or 'revelation' of Christ at His 2d coming (1 Pe 1:7, 13; cf. ch 4:13)" (*ibid.*).

Recognizing the Advent's Nearness

In His sermon on the Mount of Olives (Matt. 24; Mark 13; Luke 21), Christ presented a number of signs that would indicate that His coming is near, even "at the very doors" (Matt. 24:33). The disciples had asked three questions: about the timing of Jerusalem's destruction, Christ's coming, and the end of the age. Christ's reply mingled the description of these two events, giving signs for both. Other New Testament writings also offer signs of the closeness of the Second Coming.

Signs would appear among the sun, moon, and stars (Matt. 24:29, 30; Luke 21:25; Rev. 6:12, 13); wars, rumors of war, fear, famine, and disaster would afflict the human race (Matt. 24:6, 7; Luke 21:11, 25, 26; Joel 3:9-14; Rev. 11:18). People would have to endure a time of trouble such as the human race has never experienced before (Dan. 12:1). False christs and false prophets would claim to speak for God (Matt. 24:4, 5, 11, 23-27). Earthquakes, pestilence, and storms would rage across the face of the earth (Matt. 24:7; Luke 21:11). Lawlessness and sin would rival the days of Noah (Matt. 24:12; Luke 17:26-30; 2 Tim. 3:1-5, 13). Capital and labor disputes would rock the economic world (James 5:1-6). People would scoff at the thought of Christ returning again (2 Peter 3:1-4). Spiritualism would spread (1 Tim. 4:1, 2).

Doubt and apostasy will arise in the church. "Preach the word! . . . For the time will come when they will not endure sound doctrine, but according to their own desires, because they have itching ears, they will heap up for themselves teachers; and they will turn their ears away from the truth, and be turned aside to fables" (2 Tim. 4:2-4; cf. 2 Peter 2:1, 2; Luke 18:8; Matt. 24:12). The antidote for such apostasy will be to present Scripture (2 Tim. 4:2). Indeed, in the last days, understanding of the book of Daniel would increase (Dan. 12:4). In conjunction with a renewed comprehension of Daniel will be the proclamation of a judgment-hour message (Rev. 14:7), and the "gospel of the kingdom will be preached in all the world as a witness to all the nations, and then the end will come" (Matt. 24:14; cf. Matt. 28:19, 20).

Christ assures us that His promise to return would not pass away. Just as the leafing of the fig tree indicated that summer was near in Palestine, so these signs indicate that the Second Coming is approaching, even at the very doors (Matt. 24:32-35; cf. Mark 13:28-31; Luke 21:29-33).

A Glorious Event

The second advent of Christ will be a glorious event. "For the Lord Himself will descend from heaven with a shout, with the voice of an archangel, and with the trumpet of God" (1 Thess. 4:16). The Son of man will appear with power and spectacle, "and He will send His angels with a great sound of a trumpet" (Matt. 24:30, 31; cf. Mark 13:26, 27; Luke 9:26). "Christ's coming will be 'with clouds' (Rev. 1:7), 'in the clouds' (Matt. 24:30; 25:62; Mark 13:26; 14:62), or 'in a cloud' (Luke 21:27; cf. Acts 1:9; 1 Thess. 4:17); as attended by hosts of angels (Matt. 24:31; Mark 8:38; 13:27; Rev. 14:14-16). His coming is spoken of as glorious (Matt. 16:27; 24:30; 25:31; Mark 10:37; 13:26; Luke 9:26; 21:27; 1 Peter 4:13; 5:1), and is compared to a great flash of lightning that illuminates the entire heavens (Matt. 24:27; Luke 17:24)" (*Seventh-day Adventist Encyclopedia* [1996] vol. 11, p. 565). Christ will come as King of kings, and as the King of glory (Rev. 19:16).

The second coming of Christ will have no secrecy about it. It will be by far the greatest visual and audible show the earth has ever witnessed. Every eye will see Him (Matt. 24:27, 30; 25:31-46; Luke 17:24; Acts 1:9-11; 1 John 3:2; Rev. 1:7). The world will hear a shout of command and the sound of the trumpets (Matt. 24:31; 1 Thess. 4:16; 1 Cor. 15:51, 52).

At the coming of the Son of man God will reward everybody according to what they have done in life (Matt. 16:27; Rev. 22:12). The hope of the Second Coming is a promise for both the righteous living and dead. "For the Lord Himself will descend from heaven with a shout, with the voice of an archangel, and with the trumpet of God. And the dead in Christ will rise first. Then we who are alive and remain shall be caught up together with them in the clouds to meet the Lord in the air. And thus we shall always be with the Lord" (1 Thess. 4:16, 17). Paul elaborates further, "Behold, I tell you a mystery: We shall not all sleep, but we shall all be changed—in a moment, in the twinkling of an eye, at the last trumpet. For the trumpet will sound, and the dead will be raised incorruptible, and we shall be changed" (1 Cor. 15:51, 52; cf. verses 53-57). The angels will gather the "elect from the four winds, from one end of heaven to the other" (Matt. 24:31) and Christ will reward the righteous (Matt. 25:31-34; 2 Tim. 4:8; 1 Cor. 15:22).

Christ will end our evil age, for He is coming "in flaming fire taking vengeance on those who do not know God, and on those who do not obey the gospel of our Lord Jesus Christ. These shall be punished with everlasting destruction from the presence of the Lord and from the glory of His power" (2 Thess. 1:8, 9; cf. Rev. 6:15-17; Matt. 25:46).

While the Second Coming will take place with great fanfare and drama, we must be careful not to depersonalize it. It is Christ who is returning—not only the God of the universe who created all things. The same Jesus who ascended into heaven—our Saviour and friend—will return for us (Acts 1:11). He who once dwelt among us will come back to take us home with Him (John 17:3).

Always Be Ready

But we have waited a long time. Does it seem as if the signs of Christ's coming have already been fulfilled? If so, has God forgotten His promise? Peter explores this question: "The Lord is not slack concerning His promise, as some count slackness, but is longsuffering toward us, not willing that any should perish but that all should come to repentance" (2 Peter 3:9).

When a colleague of mine heard that I was writing a book on the Second Coming, she asked, "Do you have any special insight? I would like to know when He is coming!"

"It has been revealed to me that He is coming in the year 2006 on July 17 at 3:49 a.m. Eastern Standard Time," I joked.

We chuckled together for a moment, then she said, "Really, I have so much to do. I am a time-driven person and would like to know when He is coming!"

Christ gave us several parables illustrating the need to be ready whenever He arrives. If the householder had known at what time a thief would break in, he would have stayed awake and not allowed the burglar to break in (Matt. 24:43). Another man leaves a servant in charge of his household who then reasons, "My master is delaying his coming; therefore, I will slack off on my responsibility, and eat and drink with the drunkards" (see verses 45-49). A third parable relates the story of 10 bridesmaids who wait for the bridegroom to come back from the bride's home with her. Five of the bridesmaids were wise and took extra oil for their lamp, knowing that there was no set time in Palestine for the bridegroom to arrive and that it was contrary to custom for him to hurry back anyway. The other five took no additional oil. The girls slumbered while awaiting the arrival of the groom, and their lamps went out. The five foolish bridesmaids could not enter with the wedding party (Matt. 25:1-12). The lesson from all these parables is "Watch . . . , for you know neither the day nor the hour in which the Son of Man is coming" (Matt. 25:13; cf. Luke 21:31-36).

Is God playing tricks on us by delaying His coming? Is He trying to catch us off guard when He does arrive? Christ is returning for His own—for those who have entered a relationship with Him. Those who are living in fellowship with God are ready for His coming—in fact, heaven has already begun for them. But those who shun fellowship with God will be unprepared for His advent, because they would not be comfortable living in His presence.

The second coming of Christ is a glorious occasion, one to look forward to with expectation. The book of Hebrews says that Christ is returning the second time for those who eagerly wait for Him (Heb. 9:28). Isaiah said: "Behold, this is our God; we have waited for Him, and He will save us" (Isa. 25:9). Paul looked "for the blessed hope and glorious appearing of our great God and Savior Jesus Christ" (Titus 2:13). Even in his time of trouble, Job exclaimed, "How my heart yearns within me!" (Job 19:27). God does not want us to live in fear and trembling as we contemplate His soon return. Relationships do not thrive on fear. John assures us, "Abide in Him, that when He appears, we may have confidence" (1 John 2:28).

Peter asks a serious question. What kind of people ought we to be in view of the second coming of Christ? He admonishes us to "be diligent to be found by Him in peace, without spot and blameless" (2 Peter 3:14). Paul also emphasizes holiness: "For the grace of God that brings salvation has appeared to all men, teaching us that, denying ungodliness and worldly lusts, we should live soberly, righteously, and godly in the present age, looking for the blessed hope and glorious appearing of our great God and Savior Jesus Christ, who gave Himself for us, that He might redeem us from every lawless deed and purify for Himself His own special people, zealous for good works" (Titus 2:11-14). John emphasizes that when He appears, "we shall be like Him, for we shall see Him as He is" (1 John 3:2; cf. 2 Thess. 1:10).

Why is it important for us to be like Him when He returns? Because God wants to restore us to an intimate relationship with Him. But sin and righteousness cannot have fellowship with each other. We can draw close to God as to a friend only when our character harmonizes with His.

What we think of God affects the way we live. That is why Christ said that salvation is knowing the "only true God" (John 17:3). Our characters mold themselves to the thing or person that we admire most in life. If our allegiance and admiration is for the true God, our characters will begin to reflect His. And when our characters pattern themselves after His, then our lives will harmonize with Him. Once like Him in character, we can fellowship with Him uninterrupted by the barriers of sin.

Is Christ's likeness the basis of salvation? Yes! But not our own righteousness—His righteousness, the robe of His own righteousness that He clothes us with when we accept His blood on the cross as our atonement for our sins. Often we find ourselves tempted to try to earn salvation on our own. We seek to do it our way, to give God the parameters and conditions under which He can save us. Such temptations contrast with the faith of those recorded in the biblical hall of faith, with those who lived by faith in the Word of God rather than by human might and wisdom.

God is summoning a people who are willing to live by faith in His Word and to proclaim by faith the nearness of His coming, to prepare the way of the Lord. How will you respond to God's call to play your part in announcing the glorious reunion with Christ, our Lord and Saviour? Christ says: "Surely I am coming quickly." Let us respond by saying, "Even so, come, Lord Jesus!" (Rev. 22:20).

Chapter 12

The Millennium, the Destruction of the Wicked, and the New Earth

WHEN THE Godhead planned the creation of the universe, they desired to share their love and fellowship with the created beings. They intended peace and fellowship among the inhabitants of the universe, and that all beings would live in harmony with nature. Created beings would respond to each other and to God out of love. Love cannot be forced. True love is a response from the heart. Since God did not desire the affection of automatons; He created a universe in which the creature had freedom to choose whether to live in harmony with God's character.

Unfortunately, Satan took advantage of that fact by choosing to oppose God. He led one third of the angels to follow him, and convinced the human race to join him outside of the confines of the Word of God. Sin had disrupted God's original plan, resulting in chaos, sorrow, and death. As ruler of the universe, God took responsibility to provide a setting of happiness for His creatures. He quickly went into action with His fall-back plan to restore humanity to a right relationship with Him, and to reestablish peace in the universe.

God can do that only through the total destruction of sin and everything associated with it. Further, He desires to solve the sin problem in such a way that sin will not surface a second time. Let us follow God's plan from the Second Coming to the destruction of sin and the wicked so that we might understand what He has in mind.

This period of time we often call the millennium (1,000

years). While "millennium" does not occur in the Bible, Revelation 20:1-7 speaks of a 1,000-year period six times. We will look at the events before, during, and after the millennium in order to grasp how God intends to restore peace in the universe.

The Beginning of the Millennium

The second coming of Christ occurs at the beginning of the millennium. The context of Revelation 20 is the arrival of the King of kings and Lord of lords with the armies of heaven to destroy the wicked (Rev. 19:11-16). Our last chapter noted that two classes of people would exist at the Second Advent. Christ describes the scene: "When the Son of Man comes in His glory, and all the holy angels with Him, then He will sit on the throne of His glory. All the nations will be gathered before Him, and He will separate them one from another, as a shepherd divides his sheep from the goats. And He will set the sheep on His right hand, but the goats on the left. Then the King will say to those on His right hand, 'Come, you blessed of My Father, inherit the kingdom prepared for you from the foundation of the world.' . . . Then He will also say to those on the left hand, 'Depart from Me, you cursed, into the everlasting fire prepared for the devil and his angels'" (Matt. 25:31-41).

The wicked will attempt to hide from Christ (Rev. 19:15-19; 6:14-17), but they will be slain (Rev. 19:20, 21), for Christ's glory will consume them (2 Thess. 1:7-10; cf. 2 Thess. 2:8; Heb. 12:29).

Those who have lived for Christ and for the Word of God—those who have not worshiped the beast or his image, or had his mark in the forehead or hand—will rise in the first resurrection (Rev. 20:4-6). At the same time, the living righteous will also receive immortality, and the two groups will meet Christ in the air (1 Thess. 4:16, 17; 1 Cor. 15:51-54). Christ, who has returned for His people, will then take them home to live with Him (John 14:1-3).

During the Millennium

At this point the earth is desolate, for the wicked have perished and the righteous have gone to heaven. Satan will then be

MILLENNIUM—WICKED—NEW EARTH

bound, confined to the earth, or the bottomless pit, so that he cannot deceive the nations until the 1,000 years have ended (Rev. 20:1-3).

The Septuagint uses the same Greek word in Genesis 1:2 as employed here for "bottomless pit." The earth will return to the state described as without form and void on the first day of Creation (cf. 2 Peter 3:10). Ellen White portrays the scene of desolation after the Second Coming:

"The earth looked like a desolate wilderness. Cities and villages, shaken down by the earthquake, lay in heaps. Mountains had been moved out of their places, leaving large caverns. . . . Here is to be the home of Satan with his evil angels for a thousand years. Here he will be confined, to wander up and down over the broken surface of the earth and see the effects of his rebellion against God's law. For a thousand years he can enjoy the fruit of the curse which he has caused. Limited alone to the earth, he will not have the privilege of ranging to other planets, to tempt and annoy those who have not fallen. During this time, Satan suffers extremely. Since his fall his evil traits have been in constant exercise. But he is then to be deprived of his power, and left to reflect upon the part which he has acted since his fall, and to look forward with trembling and terror to the dreadful future, when he must suffer for all the evil that he has done and be punished for all the sins that he has caused to be committed" (*Early Writings,* p. 290).

During the 1,000 years between the first and the second resurrections, the righteous will actively participate in the judgment of the wicked. "The apostle Paul points to this judgment as an event that follows the second advent. 'Judge nothing before the time, until the Lord come, who both will bring to light the hidden things of darkness, and will make manifest the counsels of the hearts.' 1 Corinthians 4:5. Daniel declares that when the Ancient of Days came, 'judgment was given to the saints of the Most High.' Daniel 7:22. At this time the righteous reign as kings and priests unto God. John in the Revelation says: 'I saw thrones, and they sat upon them, and judgment was given unto them.' 'They shall be priests of God and of Christ, and shall reign with Him a thousand years.' Revelation 20:4, 6. It is at this time that, as foretold by Paul, 'the saints shall judge the world.' 1 Corinthians 6:2. In union with Christ they judge the wicked, comparing their acts with the statute book, the Bible, and deciding every case according to the deeds done in the body. Then the portion which the wicked must suffer is meted out, according to their works; and it is recorded against their names in the book of death" (*The Great Controversy,* pp. 660, 661).

The End of the Millennium

At the end of the 1,000 years John "saw the holy city, New Jerusalem, coming down out of heaven from God, prepared as a bride adorned for her husband" (Rev. 21:2). While Revelation 21 includes this description of the descent of the New Jerusalem in the vision about the new earth, it is apparent that the city has already come to earth by the end of the millennium recorded in chapter 20, for the resurrected wicked surround it (Rev. 20:9). "The saints will rest in the Holy City and reign as kings and priests one thousand years; then Jesus will descend with the saints upon the Mount of Olives, and the mount will part asunder and become a mighty plain for the Paradise of God to rest upon" (*Early Writings,* p. 51).

God raises the unrighteous dead at the end of the millennium. Both Christ and Paul taught a resurrection from the dead for the wicked (John 5:28, 29; Acts 24:15). The book of Revelation specifies it as occurring at the end of the 1,000 years (Rev. 20:5, 6). Satan, who has been waiting impatiently during the millennium, now once again has opportunity to tempt others (verses 7, 8). God, who had bound him at the beginning of the millennium (verses 2, 3), now frees him to conduct his final deception. Satan marshals the forces of the resurrected wicked. They besiege the city, thinking to take it (verses 8, 9). Then fire comes down from God out of heaven and devours them. It is the second death (verses 9, 14, 15; Rev. 21:8; cf. 2 Peter 3:13).

Ellen White depicts the scene as follows: "I saw that Satan was 'loosed out of his prison,' at the end of the 1000 years, just at the time the wicked dead were raised; and that Satan deceived them by making them believe that they could take the Holy City from the saints. The wicked all marched up around the 'camp of the saints,' with Satan at their head; and when they were ready to make an effort to take the city, the Almighty breathed from His high throne, on the city, a breath of devouring fire, which came down on them, and burnt them up, 'root and branch'" (*A Word to the "Little Flock,"* pp. 11, 12). "Then the wicked saw what they had lost; and fire was breathed from God upon them, and consumed them. This was the execution of the judgment. The wicked then received according as the saints, in unison with Jesus, had meted out to them during the one thousand years. The same fire from God that consumed the wicked purified the whole earth. The broken, ragged mountains melted with fervent heat, the atmosphere also, and all the stubble was consumed. Then our inheritance opened before us, glorious and beautiful, and we inherited the whole earth made new. We all shouted with a loud voice, Glory, Alleluia" (*A Sketch of the Christian Experience and Views of Ellen G. White,* p. 45; cf. 2 Peter 3:10, 12, 13; Rev. 21:1).

Peter alludes to the same scene: "Therefore, since all these things will be dissolved, what manner of persons ought you to be in holy conduct and godliness, looking for and hastening the coming of the day of God, because of which the heavens will be dissolved, being on fire, and the elements will melt with fervent heat? Nevertheless we, according to His promise, look for new heavens and a new earth in which righteousness dwells" (2 Peter 3:11-13).

The New Earth

John saw "a new heaven and a new earth, for the first heaven and the first earth had passed away" (Rev. 21:1). The Creator will make all things new. "God will wipe away every tear from their eyes; there shall be no more death, nor sorrow, nor crying. There shall be no more pain, for the former things have passed away" (verses 4, 5; cf. 7:14-17). The river of life, issuing from the throne of God, will flow through the city. On either side of the river is the tree of life with its healing properties. No night will darken the New Jerusalem, nor will it need a sun, for God gives its inhabitants light (Rev. 21:23; 22:1-5).

Several Old Testament passages depict what Israel might have experienced had she been faithful to God. They foreshadow the new earth described in the book of Revelation. "'The righteous shall inherit the land, and dwell in it forever'" (Ps. 37:29). "'They shall build houses and inhabit them; they shall plant vineyards and eat the fruit of them. . . . The wolf and the lamb shall feed together, the lion shall eat straw like the ox. . . . They shall not hurt nor destroy in all My holy mountain,' says the Lord" (Isa. 65:21-25; cf. John 14:2; Heb. 11:13-16). Paul exclaims: "Eye has not seen, nor ear heard, nor have entered into the heart of man the things which God has prepared for those who love Him" (1 Cor. 2:9).

Life in the New Earth

Ellen White portrays life in the new earth as an active and creative one in which we develop our God-given abilities to the fullest: "There, immortal minds will contemplate with never-failing delight the wonders of creative power, the mysteries of redeeming love. There will be no cruel, deceiving foe to tempt to forgetfulness of God. Every faculty will be developed, every capacity increased. The acquirement of knowledge will not weary the mind or exhaust the energies. There the grandest enterprises may be carried forward, the loftiest aspirations reached, the highest ambitions realized; and still there will arise new heights to surmount, new wonders to admire, new truths to comprehend, fresh objects to call forth the powers of mind and soul and body.

"All the treasures of the universe will be open to the study of God's redeemed. Unfettered by mortality, they wing their tireless flight to worlds afar—worlds that thrilled with sorrow at the spectacle of human woe and rang with songs of gladness at the tidings of a ransomed soul. With unutterable delight the children of earth enter into the joy and the wisdom of unfallen beings. They share the treasures of knowledge and understanding gained through ages upon ages in contemplation of God's handiwork. With undimmed vision they gaze upon the glory of creation—suns and stars and systems, all in their appointed order circling the throne of Deity. Upon all things, from the least to the greatest, the Creator's name is written, and in all are the riches of His power displayed" (*The Great Controversy*, pp. 677, 678).

As we contemplate the beauties of heaven, its serene environment, and our ability to use our God-given resources and talents in ways never before possible, we must not forget the main point about the new earth—God and His Son, Jesus Christ, are there. Christ is coming to take us home to Himself, that we might always be where He is (John 14:1-3). The new earth will have no temple (Rev. 21:22), because it will not need any. "Behold, the tabernacle of God is with men, and He will dwell with them, and they shall be His people. God Himself will be with them and be their God" (verse 3). The Lamb Himself will shepherd us and lead us to living fountains of waters (Rev. 7:17). The Creator of the universe will be our God, and we shall be His children (Rev. 21:7).

Who will be there? Not the cowardly, unbelievers, abominable, murderers, sexually immoral, sorcerers, idolaters, and liars, who shall have perished in the lake of fire—but those who have overcome (verses 7, 8). And they shall see the face of God. His name (character) will be in their foreheads (Rev. 3:12; 21:7). Refusing to bow to the designer gods of Babylon, they have washed their robes in the blood of the Lamb, allowing God to give them a new heart. He has transformed them into His likeness. They have the privilege of living with God Himself, for they have accepted His Word as their foundation and guide. Christ has told them, "Well done, good and faithful servant. . . . Enter into the joy of your lord" (Matt. 25:21).

Designer Gods and the Death of the Wicked

We now begin to see the significance of the three angels' messages—the proclamation of the everlasting gospel, the whole truth about God. Only those who accept the God who reveals Himself can fellowship with Him. That is why the warnings of Revelation 14 are so ominous. Many misconceptions about the way God plans to end the sin problem exist. When we try to tell God how to run His universe, it puts us out of harmony with Him, and thus out of fellowship with Him.

For example, some attempt to carve out a philosophical "de-

THE CERTAINTY OF THE SECOND COMING

signer god" who escapes responsibility for the death of the wicked. They argue that wrath is not a characteristic of God, for that would hardly suit a "designer god" in an age of love. The death of the wicked is not God's doing, but simply the natural result of evil entering His presence. Such a theory thereby spares God the "guilt" of destroying the wicked. The responsibility lies with nature. Any wickedness that comes in contact with such a display of glory simply ceases to exist.

These arguments certainly create a God with whom we can be comfortable—a fashionable deity for our sophisticated society. Let us examine them to see if they work, and how they match up with the God who has revealed Himself. First of all, they imply that nature is outside of God's design and control. However, if God either designed or controls nature, then He is responsible for anything it does. On the other hand, if God Himself is bound by nature, so that He can act only in accordance with its principles, then we must question whether God is really ruler of the universe.

But the more serious objection to this designer god is that it is an idol of our own making rather than depicting the deity who has revealed Himself. Like it or not, we are not in control of who God is. It is not our place to tell Him how He should run His universe. Both Scripture and Ellen White clearly teach that God Himself takes responsibility for the destruction of the wicked (notice, not simply sin but also sinners), and that the annihilation of sinners is His act. "Behold, the day of the Lord comes, cruel, with both wrath and fierce anger, to lay the land desolate; and He will destroy its sinners from it" (Isa. 13:9; cf. verse 13; Nahum 1:3). "The great day of the Lord is near. . . . That day is a day of wrath, a day of trouble and distress, a day of devastation and desolation, a day of darkness and gloominess, a day of clouds and thick darkness" (Zeph. 1:14, 15). The message of the three angels also includes a warning about the wrath of God: "If anyone worships the beast and his image, and receives his mark on his forehead or on his hand, he himself shall also drink of the wine of the wrath of God, which is poured out full strength into the cup of His indignation. He shall be tormented with fire and brimstone in the presence of the holy angels and in the presence of the Lamb. And the smoke of their torment ascends for-

MILLENNIUM—WICKED—NEW EARTH

ever and ever; and they have no rest day or night, who worship the beast and his image, and whoever receives the mark of his name" (Rev. 14:9-11; cf. verses 19, 20; 19:15).

Some would interpret such passages to mean that the Father is a God of wrath, but that the Son, Jesus Christ, is a deity of love. However, notice that the Bible does not make such a distinction. "And the kings of the earth, the great men, the rich men, the commanders, the mighty men, every slave and every free man, hid themselves in the caves and in the rocks of the mountains, and said to the mountains and rocks, 'Fall on us and hide us from the face of Him who sits on the throne and from the wrath of the Lamb! For the great day of His wrath has come, and who is able to stand?'" (Rev. 6:15-17). The message of the third angel quoted above states that the wrath of God is poured out in the presence of the Lamb (Rev. 14:10).

The Godhead revealed the entire plan of salvation so that we might escape divine wrath. "He who believes in the Son has everlasting life; and he who does not believe the Son shall not see life, but the wrath of God abides on him" (John 3:36). But God demonstrates His own love toward us through the fact that Christ died for us while we were still sinners. "Much more then, having now been justified by His blood, we shall be saved from wrath through Him" (Rom. 5:9; cf. 1 Thess. 1:10).

Ellen White affirms that while God's destruction of the wicked is a strange act for Him, it is nonetheless His doing (*The Great Controversy*, p. 627). "The long-suffering of God is wonderful, because He puts constraint on His own attributes; but punishment is nonetheless certain. Every century of profligacy has treasured up wrath against the day of wrath; and when the time comes, and the iniquity is full, then God will do His strange work. It will be found a terrible thing to have worn out the divine patience; for the wrath of God will fall so singly and strongly that it is represented as being unmixed with mercy; and the very earth will be desolated" (*Selected Messages*, book 2, pp. 372, 373). God's wrath will flow upon those who refuse a "thus saith the Lord" and place human concepts above God's law (*This Day With God*, p. 84).

Also Ellen White reaffirms the scriptural teaching that we escape divine wrath only through Jesus' blood. "Christ was to take the wrath of God which in justice should fall upon man. He became a refuge for man, and although man was indeed a criminal, deserving the wrath of God, yet he could by faith in Christ run into the refuge provided and be safe. In the midst of death there was life if man chose to accept it" (*Review and Herald,* Feb. 24, 1874). Thus, although the destruction of the wicked is God's act, out of His love He has provided a way by which we might escape eternal destruction. His desire is that we might have life!

Designer Gods and the Doctrine of Hell

On the other side of the spectrum are those who have no problem recognizing the destruction of the wicked as a divine act, but who also teach that God will torture sinners with the fires of hell for eternity. They build upon several Bible passages that we can misinterpret to refer to an eternally tormenting hellfire: "everlasting fire," (Matt. 25:41), "eternal fire" (Jude 7), and smoke ascending "forever and ever" (Rev. 14:11). It is important to take the Bible as a whole, and to allow it to be its own interpreter. "A study of the usage and meaning of the Greek term *aiōnios,* as used in connection with the fire of the last days, shows that the emphasis is on its destructiveness rather than on its duration. For example, Sodom and Gomorrah met with the punishment of eternal (*aiōnios*) fire (Jude 7). The fire completely destroyed these cities, but became extinct long centuries ago. Jude set forth the destruction of these cities as an 'example' of the fate that awaited the licentious apostates of his day. The term 'unquenchable' may be similarly understood. Jeremiah predicted that God would kindle a fire in the gates of Jerusalem that would 'not be quenched' (Jer. 17:27). This prediction was fulfilled when the city was destroyed by Nebuchadnezzar (ch 52:12, 13; cf. Neh. 1:3). Obviously that fire is not burning today. Clearly the meaning is that it would not be quenched but would thoroughly destroy" (*Seventh-day Adventist Bible Dictionary* [1979], p. 475. For further discussion, see also pp. 277, 278, 347).

The Bible does not teach that the wicked will live on, tormented forever in hellfire. Scripture reveals that the wicked will be destroyed and cease to exist. "'And the day which is coming shall burn them up,' says the Lord of hosts, 'that will leave them neither root nor branch'" (Mal. 4:1). The wicked will be "devoured" (Rev. 20:9; Ps. 21:9; Heb. 10:27) and "destroyed" (Ps. 145:20; 2 Thess. 1:9). "Nothing" of them shall survive (Isa. 41:11, 12).

These two doctrines—that God does not personally destroy the wicked, and the concept that the wicked will eternally endure torture in hell—demonstrate the importance of accepting God just as He has revealed Himself in the Bible. The teaching that God does not destroy the wicked raises questions about His nature and role in the universe. Is God a deity of love only, and not also of justice? Is God Himself subject to nature's laws? How often people say about something, "That does not conform to my idea of God." Is my idea of God really the criterion for Him? Am I uncomfortable with a God who destroys the wicked? And if I am, does that give me the right to tell Him that He cannot participate in their destruction? Do I say to Him, "God, stand aside and let nature take its course"?

At the opposite end is the danger of misunderstanding the character of God by teaching an eternally tormenting hellfire. Ellen White states that "it is beyond the power of the human mind to estimate the evil which has been wrought by the heresy of eternal torment. The religion of the Bible, full of love and goodness, and abounding in compassion, is darkened by superstition and clothed with terror. When we consider in what false colors Satan has painted the character of God, can we wonder that our merciful Creator is feared, dreaded, and even hated? The appalling views of God which have spread over the world from the teachings of the pulpit have made thousands, yes, millions, of skeptics and infidels" (*The Great Controversy*, p. 536).

The doctrine of the immortality of the soul leads many to the idea of universal salvation. "A large class to whom the doctrine of eternal torment is revolting are driven to the opposite error. They see that the Scriptures represent God as a being of love and compassion, and they cannot believe that He will consign His creatures to the fires of an eternally burning hell. But holding that the soul is naturally immortal, they see no alternative but to conclude that all mankind will finally be saved. Many regard the threatenings of the Bible as designed merely to frighten men into obedience, and not to be literally fulfilled. Thus the sinner can live in selfish pleasure, disregarding the requirements of God, and yet expect to be finally received into His favor. Such a doctrine, presuming upon God's mercy, but ignoring His justice, pleases the carnal heart and emboldens the wicked in their iniquity" (*ibid.,* p. 537).

The theory of eternal torment is one of the false doctrines that constitute the wine of Babylon. It came from paganized Christianity just as did the change of the day of worship from Saturday to Sunday (*ibid.,* p. 536). The Word of God is the antidote for such misleading concepts. "It is a straight chain of truth, and will prove an anchor to those who are willing to receive it, even if they have to sacrifice their cherished fables" (*Testimonies,* vol. 1, p. 345).

These two doctrines distort our view of the "only true God" who has revealed Himself to us. On the one hand, we might relate to Him in terror, while on the other, we might lose our respect for Him and therefore fail to recognize the importance of living in harmony with His law, which reflects His character. Since either concept warps our understanding of God, they also affect our relationship with Him.

The issue in the great controversy between Christ and Satan is our relationship to the Word of God. "Satan erected his standard of revolt against God in heaven. He aspired to be like God, and determined to assert a power of independence of God. His after-history has revealed a persevering determination to establish his empire, governed by laws, and replenished with resources, independent of God. Every species of idolatry, sensuality, crime, rebellion, and irreligion is the fruit borne from the proud and exalted claims of Satan" (*Review and Herald,* June 21, 1898). Thus Satan desires to tempt us to question God, and to put ourselves ahead of the Word of God. His goal is to teach us to live in independence from God.

Those who have followed Satan would not be happy in heaven. They have never learned its language. "A life of rebellion against God has unfitted them for heaven. Its purity, holiness, and peace would be torture to them; the glory of God would be a consuming fire. They would long to flee from that holy place. They would welcome destruction, that they might be hidden from the face of Him who died to redeem them. The destiny of the wicked is fixed by their own choice. Their exclusion from heaven is voluntary with themselves, and just and merciful on the part of God" (*The Great Controversy*, p. 543).

"The whole wicked world stand arraigned at the bar of God on the charge of high treason against the government of heaven. They have none to plead their cause; they are without excuse; and the sentence of eternal death is pronounced against them.

"It is now evident to all that the wages of sin is not noble independence and eternal life, but slavery, ruin, and death. The wicked see what they have forfeited by their life of rebellion. The far more exceeding and eternal weight of glory was despised when offered them; but how desirable it now appears. 'All this,' cries the lost soul, 'I might have had; but I chose to put these things far from me. Oh, strange infatuation! I have exchanged peace, happiness, and honor for wretchedness, infamy, and despair.' All see that their exclusion from heaven is just. By their lives they have declared: 'We will not have this Man [Jesus] to reign over us.'

"As if entranced, the wicked have looked upon the coronation of the Son of God. They see in His hands the tables of the divine law, the statutes which they have despised and transgressed. They witness the outburst of wonder, rapture, and adoration from the saved; and as the wave of melody sweeps over the multitudes without the city, all with one voice exclaim, 'Great and marvellous are thy works, Lord God Almighty; just and true are thy ways, thou King of saints' (Rev. 15:3); and, falling prostrate, they worship the Prince of life" (*ibid.*, pp. 668, 669).

The controversy has ended. At the name of Jesus every knee shall bow, and every tongue shall confess that Jesus is Christ, Lord of heaven and earth! Amen.

Chapter 13

God Reveals His Righteousness

THE TIME has finally come. It is the greatest event ever to take place in the history of the universe, and you are there. In fact, every inhabitant of the universe who has ever lived is present. The hustle and bustle of the crowd is unbelievable. Such excitement! Greeting old friends whom you lost to death years ago, and meeting new friends, even some who lived thousands of years ago—the rich and famous as well as those not so fortunate.

The setting is like a Greek amphitheater, only immeasurably larger, and shaped in a semicircle with risers so that all can see. The acoustics are superb. One can hear a pin dropped at the center of the stage even in the highest bleacher.

Suddenly someone steps onto the stage. A distinguished man attempts to hush the crowd. Others in the bleachers join in bringing order to the occasion. As the crowd settles down, rumors spread that the man on the stage is Napoleon,[1] the famous general and former emperor of France. He takes several steps forward with a stride that manifests his composure and pride. Dead silence greets him as he begins to speak. "We are here for a very important occasion. This is not the trial of the year or decade, or even of the millennium. We are here for the trial of the ages—the trial of God. Yes, God is on trial. We would like to know if He is worthy to be God. We will examine His actions to determine whether or not He has acted wisely, whether He has preserved liberty and peace, whether He has acted in love and with justice.

"Our first task will be to determine what truth is so that we can have a basis for judging God. We will extrapolate principles of truth from our study of nature, history, and interpersonal relationships—the principles by which the universe operates. Then will come the time for the truth about God. If He abides by these universal principles, then we can make a rational judgment in His favor, and the universe can safely worship Him.

"The jury—well, that's you. You will decide. The prosecuting attorney—that's you also. And the judge—well, that is in your hands as well. And now, ladies and gentlemen—oh, and the angelic host, you are welcome also! As I was saying, we must go to great lengths to make sure that we are fair with God. We must examine all of the evidence and test it against the principles of freedom, truth, justice, and love—the foundational principles of the universe. When we are finished, we want to make sure that we have a clear basis upon which to judge God, because we would like to have a 100 percent consensus on our decision. Does that sound fair enough?" The crowd responds with a loud applause, quickly standing to their feet as the ovation continues. Napoleon takes a bow. Stretching out his arms, he then lowers them, signaling for the crowd to settle down again.

"Well, then," Napoleon continues, "I suggest that in the style of the best of democracy, we choose a chairman—I mean, a chairperson—to guide us through this process. I recommend that we nominate a general to fill this function. After all, generals are powerful individuals. Knowing how to persuade and organize people, they can bring order out of chaos. With such a large group here, I believe we will need just such a person. I would like to suggest for nomination Alexander the Great, that mighty Greek general who consolidated an even larger empire than mine."

Nero, emperor of Rome, immediately stands to his feet, exclaiming, "Why would you choose Alexander? I was the emperor of the great Roman Empire that conquered Greece. I nominate myself, thank you!"

Napoleon again proudly steps forward. "There will be no self-nominations. You must come to this task with greater humility. Otherwise, obviously, I would have chosen myself."

"Alexander is surely a great man, but he has too many enemies," a voice protests. "He can hardly bring consensus. Actually, that would be the problem with any general. Let's move on to an-

THE CERTAINTY OF THE SECOND COMING

other candidate." The crowd clearly agrees with the suggestion.

Napoleon seems somewhat disturbed that they have so readily dismissed his candidate, but he quickly regains his composure and asks, "All right, any other suggestions?" as he scans the vast audience for hands.

George Bernard Shaw immediately stands to his feet. "We need a playwright, someone who understands human nature and the game of life, who knows how to act it out, so that we can grasp the issues more readily. I nominate Shakespeare!" Immediately it seems as if people everywhere are jumping to their feet to make nominations.

Another voice comes from near the back. "We should consider someone who really grasps the human spirit. Someone who knows how to capture the imagination and the heart. Someone who can move to action. I can think of no one other than the musician—"

An immediate rebuff springs up from an artist. "I understand what you are trying to say," he says. "But really, art is the medium that best depicts the breadth of the human spirit. I nominate—" But before he can finish, a poet leaps to her feet. "I really wonder where common sense has gone. Everyone knows that poetry can get to the heart of things faster than any other of the arts. A poet will surely carry us along with the spirit of this occasion better than anyone else. I nominate—"

A rumbling begins among that portion of the crowd from the eighteenth century and on, the era of the Enlightenment and of science. Sir Francis Bacon, a famous scientist, manages to get the attention of the vast throng. "I have been amazed at how far the scientific revolution has taken us. Science is king. The foundation of discovery and knowledge, it has performed miracles of healing, provided mass travel and communication, discovered vast sources of energy, and allowed us to explore the depths of the seas and the outer reaches of space. We need a scientist who has the ability to synthesize all of this vast scientific knowledge, who can not only see the trees, but also survey the forest. This will give us the best foundation for our knowledge and thus for our verdict about God. I nominate Darwin, whose magnum opus has dominated scientific thinking right down to the present."

The philosopher Plato slowly stands and somehow manages to capture the attention of the assembly. "Since my resurrection I have been amazed at the latest accomplishments of science. I understand as well the need to grasp the human spirit, and I support the effort to find an organizing principle for knowledge. But it is the task of philosophy, not of science, to integrate all of the human disciplines. I nominate Socrates, the father of philosophy and of human thought. Who else can take the chair with such brilliance of mind, such agility of spirit, and such command of the situation? Surely he is best qualified to guide us in the discovery process to a fair verdict; one that we can all assent to."

Since his resurrection, Socrates has already made a number of friends. He has visited with distinguished leaders from all eras of human history—with philosophers, scientists, politicians, and those who have contributed to the arts. He has already become well known for his openness and breadth and agility of mind. As Aristotle rises to second the motion, you can sense relief and agreement that they have at last found the right person.

Socrates accepts the position with some hesitation. Slowly as he descends the stairs to take his position, the crowd stands to its feet with applause. As he brings the assembly back to order, he is obviously in deep thought. Then he begins. "Our work is surely the most important task that has ever been undertaken in the history of the universe. We must be fair yet thorough. To do that, we need to study God's actions in all ages to make sure that He has been fair and honest, and has always acted out of love, justice, and with truth. It would take eternity for this assembly to undertake such a study. Therefore, I suggest that we break into subcommittees representative of different eras, geographic locations, and scholarly specialties so that we can carefully look at things from every angle."

The Nature of Knowledge

"However, before we break into committees, I think that it is important for us to agree on several questions. What is knowledge? What is truth, love, and justice? Then we must decide what principles will guide us in determining whether God has acted in harmony in each area."

THE CERTAINTY OF THE SECOND COMING

Plato[2] immediately rises to his feet. "I am so pleased that you have accepted my nomination, Socrates. I knew you would immediately get to the nub of things. I have given a lot of thought to this question of knowledge. It is quite self-evident that knowledge does not primarily come from the things we apprehend with our senses—touch, taste, sight, hearing, smell, etc.—but rather from what emanates to the mind from eternal forms. This is what enables us to integrate what we observe with our senses into knowledge. For example, it is the concept of the triangle that enables us to recognize a specific instance of a triangle."

You can tell that Socrates, though somewhat disturbed at this suggestion, acts very quickly to regain control of himself. "I recall our student-teacher days with fondness, Plato. Certainly you will remember that we determined that knowledge is first of all innate, that we are already born with it, that we have only to discover it by means of dialogue."

Already you see the intellectual boxing match under way as Aristotle presents his rebuttal and alternate suggestion. "As my predecessors and teachers, I have high esteem for both of you. However, I must respectfully disagree. Knowledge is really a little more concrete than what you are suggesting. What we carefully observe with our senses is absolutely essential to knowledge."

Descartes is next in line. His question is more fundamental. "How do we know that we know anything at all? How do I know that you exist? In fact, how do I know that I exist, that I am not simply the figment of some imagination?"

"You fellows from Greece," Kant protests, "are assuming that there is a definite stable reality that is available to my mind that I can call knowledge. But in actuality, I cannot know anything for sure outside of myself, for my mind could be distorting what I see as reality outside of me. There is no way that I can get outside of my mind to determine that there is any congruence between what I think I see and what is actually out there. If we really wish to judge God, we must turn inside ourselves, to our moral nature. That will give us the proper set of principles for coming to a verdict on God."

Finally Whitehead rises to his feet. "I am somewhat perplexed

GOD REVEALS HIS RIGHTEOUSNESS

by all of this discussion about knowledge. It seems that each of you has assumed that there is some definite eternal structure, whether inside or outside of us, that we can know. The only problem is this—reality itself is not static. It is in the process of evolution. In fact, God Himself is in process. If we are going to come to a verdict about God, we must decide from which era to glean the principles by which we will judge Him. We can hardly expect Him to be above the environment within which He is evolving at the time. Thus it would not be fair to use the sophisticated principles of the twenty-first century as a basis for judging what God did thousands of years ago, for reality was rather primitive back then. On second thought, maybe we can grasp the principles that are driving evolution itself, that is, if they themselves are not in the process of evolution, and we can use them as the criteria for judging God."

Pilate can hardly contain himself. "Three thousand years ago I asked the question 'What is truth?' Now finally we are getting some good discussion. But it doesn't seem as if we have made a lot of headway. Can someone please help me? What is truth?"

Lucifer steps onto the stage. "You are all doing so marvelously. I am very pleased with myself—at how well I have trained you to think critically. And as you have clearly demonstrated, things are not so clear-cut after all. We have not been able to agree among us about the nature of truth, love, or justice. But that is only natural. It is all right, for truth is really relative. There is no one given standard in the universe that we can universally agree upon with any degree of certainty. Each of us perceives truth individually, and so, really, we are accountable only to ourselves, not to anything or anyone else! We must emphasize our independence from God. Were it not for that independence, we would not be in a position to judge God as we are now doing.

"Those poor people down through the ages who have thought that they needed to live by the so-called Word of God—why, I met one of them out there in the wilderness of Judea 3,000 years ago, and look what happened to him—he was crucified, a most humiliating and cruel death. That's what he got for being so straight-laced.

"Well, I am delighted, absolutely delighted. We have brought together the most distinguished minds that the world has produced. I can hardly wait until we get to the verdict. Poor God, I wonder how He will come out! Let us ascend into heaven, and exalt ourselves above the stars of God. And 'let us also sit on the mount of the congregation on the farthest sides of the north; and ascend above the heights of the clouds, and be like the Most High' [see Isa. 14:13, 14]. Why, we could be designer gods ourselves, couldn't we! Oh, well, I didn't mean to delay the proceedings. It's just that I can hardly contain myself with the excellency of wisdom, knowledge, and judgment manifested here. Well, please get back to the trial so that we can—"

Words Without Knowledge

All of a sudden Lucifer finds himself interrupted. What is happening? A voice like the sound of thunder echoes through the amphitheater, but it is clear, distinct, and resonant. "Who is this who darkens counsel by words without knowledge? Now prepare yourself like a man; I will question you, and you shall answer Me. Where were you when I laid the foundations of the earth? Tell Me, if you have understanding. Who determined its measurements? Surely you know! Or who stretched the line upon it? To what were its foundations fastened? Or who laid its cornerstone, when the morning stars sang together, and all the sons of God shouted for joy?" (Job 38:2-7).

"Who has directed the Spirit of the Lord, or as His counselor has taught Him? With whom did He take counsel, and who instructed Him, and taught Him in the path of justice? Who taught Him knowledge, and showed Him the way of understanding? Behold, the nations are as a drop in a bucket, and are counted as the small dust on the scales; look, He lifts up the isles as a very little thing" (Isa. 40:13-15).

"To whom then will you liken God? Or what likeness will you compare to Him? The workman molds a graven image, the goldsmith overspreads it with gold, and the silversmith casts silver chains. Whoever is too impoverished for such a contribution chooses a tree that will not rot; he seeks for himself a skillful workman to prepare a carved image that will not totter. Have you not known? Have you not heard? Has it not been told you from the beginning? Have you not understood from the foundations of the earth? It is He who sits above the circle of the earth, and its inhabitants are like grasshoppers, who stretches out the heavens like a curtain, and spreads them out like a tent to dwell in. He brings the princes to nothing; he makes the judges of the earth useless" (verses 18-23).

"There is no searching of My understanding. Keep silence before Me, Lucifer! Come near for judgment. Who in righteousness has called Me to My feet? Who gave the nations to Me? Who made Me ruler over kings? I, the Lord, am the first; and with the last I am He. Your molded images are wind and confusion [see Isa. 40:28; 41:1, 2, 4, 29]. Your designer gods are just that—gods that you have made and control.

"'For My thoughts are not your thoughts, nor are your ways My ways,' says the Lord. 'For as the heavens are higher than the earth, so are My ways higher than your ways, and My thoughts than your thoughts'" (Isa. 55:8, 9).

Lucifer is speechless, and a long silence follows. Then that magnificent voice breaks it, bringing comfort to those who have served God down through the ages. "Fear not, for I am with you; be not dismayed, for I am your God. I will strengthen you, yes, I will help you. I will uphold you with My righteous right hand" (Isa. 41:10). "Behold, all those who were incensed against you shall be ashamed and disgraced; they shall be as nothing, and those who strive with you shall perish. You shall seek them and not find them—those who contended with you. Those who war against you shall be as nothing, as a nonexistent thing. For I, the Lord your God, will hold your right hand, saying to you, 'Fear not, I will help you'" (verses 11-13). "'Fear not, you worm Jacob, you men of Israel! I will help you,' says the Lord and your Redeemer, the Holy One of Israel" (verse 14).

Faith in God's Word

The stunned assembly nervously waits for someone to speak. A sigh of relief follows when someone finally steps forward. Then they see who it is—Job, radiant, energetic, thoughtful, yet humble. He raises his voice so as to be heard. "I was once in a situation like this, where I wanted to bring God into judgment. I did not understand what was happening to me. It seemed all so unfair. The loss of my beloved children and all of my earthly belongings. Then God spoke just as He did today—He revealed Himself in all of His glory, righteousness, truth, and love. I realized the futility of humanity trying to bring the Creator-God of the universe into judgment. The source of truth, love, justice, and knowledge; and here I was, a mere man, trying to find a standard by which to judge Him. Why, it was as if I were fashioning my own deity to see if God matched up. I was condemning God in order to justify myself [see Job 40:8]. I am ashamed at the arrogance of thinking that I could bring God into judgment. But I was so grateful for His self-revelation that I fell at His feet, repenting in dust and ashes, acknowledging that I had spoken out of my ignorance [see Job 42:2-6]. Gratefully I accepted His offer of salvation."

Chuckles go through the crowd as Job sits down. In a stage whisper someone comments, "A little primitive, don't you think?"

Noah's turn comes next. "God's plan for my life was rather unreasonable, I guess, as Lucifer has said. I was one of those who lived by the Word of God. God granted me a good deal of faith that sustained me through 120 years of preaching a highly unpopular message. It just did not fit with the attractive 'designer theologies' available elsewhere. The results of my preaching were discouraging. Only my family responded. And then waiting in the ark for seven days surrounded by those outside who jeered at my 'stupid' decision to enter the ark. Well, I preached my heart out, calling you to repentance. I kept the door of the ark open as long as I could. Finally it was too late to enter, for God Himself closed the door. Oh, how I mourned for friends and loved ones outside!" At this point in Noah's speech chanting begins from here and there around the amphitheater. "Noaic is archaic. Noaic is archaic." The hissing, nothing new to Noah, finally subsides as he takes his seat.

Adam and Eve take the stage next. "We are here to confess that we are responsible for the mess caused by sin. Although God created us in His image, we chose to go our own way—to live independently of God's Word, to design our own god according to what seemed reasonable to us. That fateful day by the tree we

GOD REVEALS HIS RIGHTEOUSNESS

decided to judge God and His Word and found out that He is the judge, and that we were the judged, found guilty, and banished with all of our descendants from that beautiful home. Thank God for that sacrificial lamb, the Lamb of God who takes away the sins of the world."

"The Lamb, our Saviour," someone cries out in ridicule. "Absolute foolishness. When are we going to get back to something reasonable?"

Paul can hardly wait to speak. "We have nothing of which to be ashamed! The gospel of Jesus Christ, that is what reveals the righteousness of God! [Rom. 1:16, 17]. Much of our discussion has been trying to use our wisdom to fashion a designer god who will fit our knowledge, understanding, and sensory experience. But this only makes the cross of Christ of no effect. The intellectual systems of our age consider the cross foolishness. But although it is a stumbling block to accepting the true God, it is the power and the wisdom of God for those who are saved [see 1 Cor. 1:17-25]." You can hear someone mumbling under his breath, "Hardly a man come of age!"

"Our attempt has been to search out the judgments of God by the wisdom of His creatures," Paul continues. "Consider what we have been doing in the light of who God is. 'Oh, the depth of the riches both of the wisdom and knowledge of God! How unsearchable are His judgments and His ways past finding out! "For who has known the mind of the Lord? Or who has become His counselor?" "Or who has first given to Him and it shall be repaid to him?" For of Him and through Him and to Him are all things, to whom be glory forever. Amen' [Rom. 11:33-36]."

At this point it seems that the crowd begins to get out of control. It feels as if Paul has crossed the line of any reasonableness. Regardless of the cultural perspective, what he said makes no sense. Just at the point when it seems that the audience will drag Paul away, Christ steps to the platform. "O My people, how I longed to bring you back to Myself. I have tried in every way to reach you. Outwardly you appear to be righteous, but inside you are filled with hypocrisy and lawlessness. You adorn the monuments of the prophets, saying that you would not have been partakers with

THE CERTAINTY OF THE SECOND COMING

your forefathers in the blood of the prophets. Yet you stone those who are sent to you. You have filled up the measure of guilt. Serpents, brood of vipers! How can you escape the condemnation of hell? Your house is left to you desolate [see Matt. 23:28-39]."

At this the crowds begin to roar. "Crucify Him! Crucify Him! We have no god but reason, no king but Lucifer. You are not the designer god that we have been waiting for. Away with Him, with this madness." Immediately Christ steps in to save His people by removing them to the New Jerusalem. The glory He manifests overwhelms the jeering crowd, and they momentarily fall back as though stunned.

Furious when they revives, the crowd immediately surrounds the New Jerusalem with plans to take the city (Rev. 20:9). But just as He has done so many times before, Christ reveals His majesty, glory, love, truth, and righteousness. "It is now evident to all that the wages of sin is not noble independence and eternal life, but slavery, ruin, and death. The wicked see what they have forfeited by their life of rebellion. The far more exceeding and eternal weight of glory was despised when offered them; but how desirable it now appears. 'All this,' cries the lost soul, 'I might have had; but I chose to put these things far from me. Oh, strange infatuation! I have exchanged peace, happiness, and honor for wretchedness, infamy, and despair.' All see that their exclusion from heaven is just. By their lives they have declared: 'We will not have this Man [Jesus] to reign over us'" (*The Great Controversy*, p. 668).

Pilate exclaims, "Truth was standing right before me, and I did not recognize Him! Instead of accepting Him as the way, the truth, and the life, I brought Him into judgment." Judas cries out, "He stooped down to wash my feet, but I would not let His love soften my heart. I betrayed Him because He did not fit into the picture of my designer god."

All at last plainly discern the mystery of the Incarnation and the Crucifixion, for God presents it before their mind's eye, and every condemned soul reads the character of his or her rejection of truth. All understand that they have had satanic misinterpretations and lies instead of "every word that proceeds from the mouth of God" (Matt. 4:4).

"Their lofty opinions, their human reasonings, were extolled; they declared themselves sufficient in themselves to understand divine mysteries, and they thought their own powers of discrimination were strong enough to discern truth for themselves. They fell an easy prey to Satan's subtlety, for he presented before them specious errors in human philosophy, which has an infatuation for human minds. They turned from the Source of all wisdom, and worshiped intellect. The message and the messengers of God were criticized and discarded as beneath their human, lofty ideas. The invitations of mercy were made a jest, and they denied the divinity of Jesus Christ and derided the idea of His pre-existence before He assumed human nature. But the tattered shreds of human reasoning will be found to be only as ropes of sand in the great day of God" (*The Seventh-day Adventist Bible Commentary,* Ellen G. White Comments, vol. 6, p. 1069).

"As if entranced, the wicked have looked upon the coronation of the Son of God. They see in His hands the tables of the divine law, the statutes which they have despised and transgressed. They witness the outburst of wonder, rapture, and adoration from the saved; and as the wave of melody sweeps over the multitudes without the city, all with one voice exclaim, 'Great and marvelous are thy works, Lord God Almighty; just and true are thy ways, thou King of saints' (Rev. 15:3); and, falling prostrate, they worship the Prince of life" (*The Great Controversy,* pp. 668, 669).

Satan himself is spellbound as he beholds Christ's glory and majesty. He sees that his voluntary rebellion has unfitted him for heaven. Constrained to acknowledge God's justice, he bows to Christ's supremacy. Yet He remains unchanged and attempts to initiate one last desperate struggle against the King of heaven (*ibid.,* pp. 670-672). God then steps in as fire comes down from God out of heaven and devours them (Rev. 20:9). Out of the ashes, God creates a new heaven and a new earth (Rev. 21:1).

The End or the Beginning?

Perhaps at this point you pause a moment, thinking back over your own life and the decisions you have made for God. Do you remember a book that you shared with another on the cer-

THE CERTAINTY OF THE SECOND COMING

tainty of the Second Coming, and perhaps the vow that you made to see someone in the new earth? And now you picture this scene with me. Is it all over? Or is it just beginning?

We're standing on the sea of glass with all who made the Word of God the guide of their life over every edict, every authority, every tribunal, every philosophy of a world now gone forever!

And we're there! With all who could ever truly enjoy heaven! Linking hands with those who have been long gone, we squeeze them, and then, spontaneously, through tears of joy as we look into the loving eyes of the One crucified for us, we begin to sing. Softly, then swelling into a chorus that shivers the rafters of eternity—

"Great and marvelous are Your works, Lord God Almighty! Just and true are Your ways, O King of the saints! Who shall not fear You, O Lord, and glorify Your name? For You alone are holy. For all nations shall come and worship before You, for Your judgments have been manifested" (Rev. 15:3, 4).

And it's just beginning! For "the years of eternity, as they roll, will bring richer and still more glorious revelations of God and of Christ. As knowledge is progressive, so will love, reverence, and happiness increase. The more men learn of God, the greater will be their admiration of His character. As Jesus opens before them the riches of redemption and the amazing achievements in the great controversy with Satan, the hearts of the ransomed thrill with more fervent devotion, and with more rapturous joy they sweep the harps of gold; and ten thousand times ten thousand and thousands of thousands of voices unite to swell the mighty chorus of praise.

"'And every creature which is in heaven, and on the earth, and under the earth, and such as are in the sea, and all that are in them, heard I saying, Blessing, and honor, and glory, and power, be unto Him that sitteth upon the throne, and unto the Lamb for ever and ever' (Rev. 5:13).

"The great controversy is ended. Sin and sinners are no more. The entire universe is clean. One pulse of harmony and gladness beats through the vast creation. From Him who created all flow life and light and gladness, throughout the realms of illimitable space. From the minutest atom to the greatest world, all things, animate and inanimate, in their unshadowed beauty and perfect joy, declare that God is love" (*The Great Controversy,* p. 678).

---

[1] I am not attempting to judge the historical figures I have used. Only God can do that.

[2] I have not attempted to describe in detail the many and varying concepts of knowledge. However, the examples chosen do illustrate the diversity of positions on the nature of knowledge.